ANTARCTICA
A GUIDE TO THE WILDLIFE

TONY SOPER

ILLUSTRATIONS BY
DAFILA SCOTT

Bradt Travel Guides, UK
The Globe Pequot Press, USA

Fourth edition 2004
First published 1994

Bradt Travel Guides Ltd
19 High Street, Chalfont St Peter, Bucks SL9 9QE, England.
Published in the USA by The Globe Pequot Press Inc,
246 Goose Lane, PO Box 480, Guilford, Connecticut 06437-0480

Other books in this series by Tony Soper:
The Arctic: A Guide to the Wildlife
British Isles: Wildlife of Coastal Waters

British Library Cataloguing-in-Publication Data
A catalogue record for this book is available from the British Library

ISBN-10: 1 84162 131 5
ISBN-13: 978 1 84162 131 9

Front cover: Adélie penguins (Dafila Scott)

Designed by Ian Chatterton
Formated by Pepenbury
Printed and bound in Italy by Printer Trento

Contents

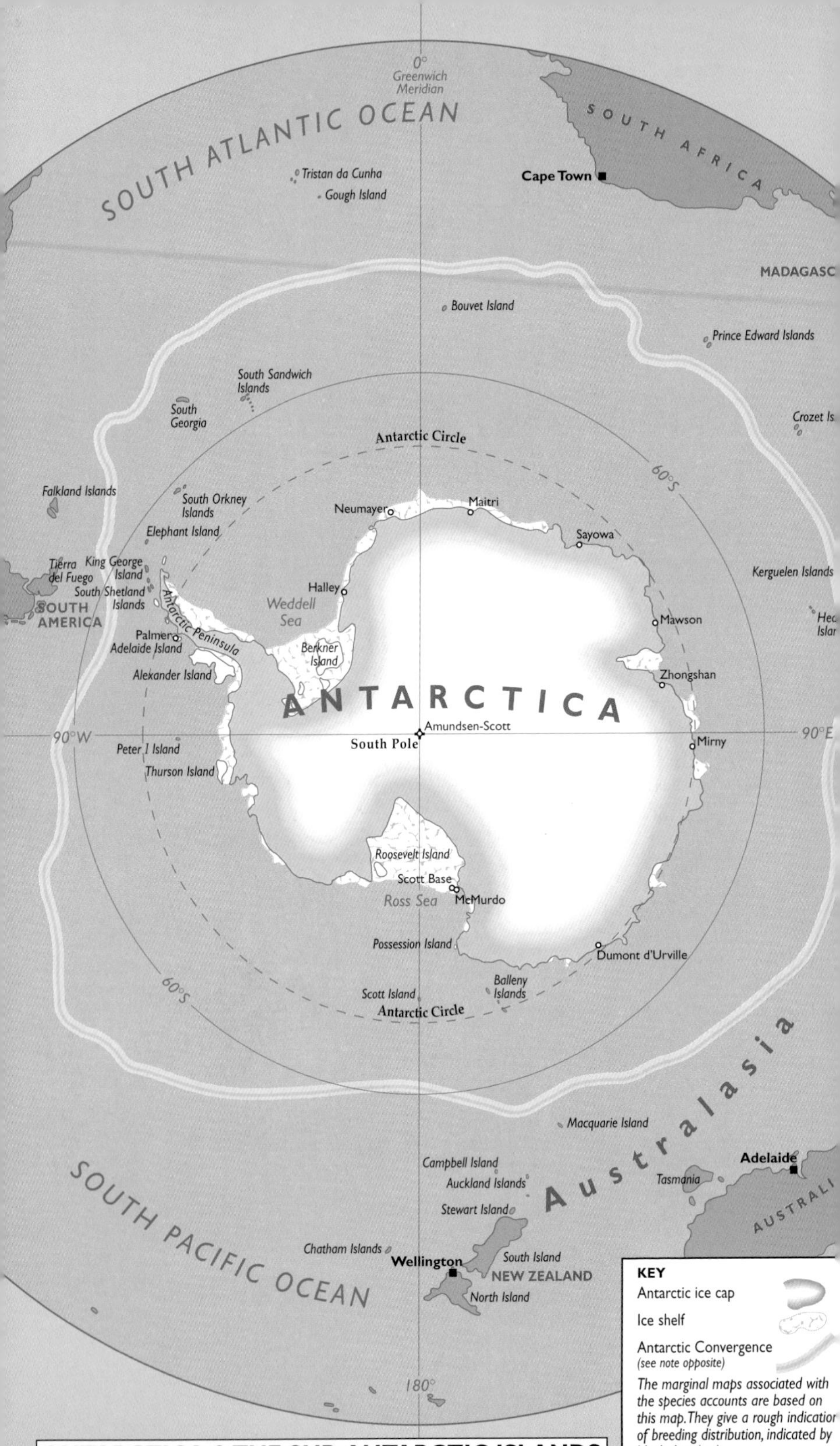
0°
Greenwich Meridian
SOUTH ATLANTIC OCEAN
SOUTH AFRICA
Cape Town
Tristan da Cunha
Gough Island
MADAGASC
Bouvet Island
Prince Edward Islands
South Sandwich Islands
South Georgia
Crozet Is
Antarctic Circle
60°S
Falkland Islands
South Orkney Islands
Elephant Island
Neumayer
Maitri
Sayowa
Tierra del Fuego
King George Island
South Shetland Islands
SOUTH AMERICA
Kerguelen Islands
Halley
Weddell Sea
Mawson
Antarctic Peninsula
Palmer
Adelaide Island
Berkner Island
Alexander Island
Zhongshan
ANTARCTICA
Amundsen-Scott
South Pole
90°W
90°E
Mirny
Peter I Island
Thurson Island
Roosevelt Island
Scott Base
McMurdo
Ross Sea
Possession Island
Dumont d'Urville
Balleny Islands
Scott Island
Antarctic Circle
60°S
Australasia
Macquarie Island
Campbell Island
Auckland Islands
Adelaide
Tasmania
AUSTRALI
Stewart Island
SOUTH PACIFIC OCEAN
Chatham Islands
South Island
Wellington
NEW ZEALAND
North Island
180°
KEY
Antarctic ice cap
Ice shelf
Antarctic Convergence
(see note opposite)
The marginal maps associated with the species accounts are based on this map. They give a rough indicatior of breeding distribution, indicated by black dots (●)

ANTARCTICA & THE SUB-ANTARCTIC ISLANDS

INTRODUCTION

Antarctica is the coldest, windiest, driest place on earth. Two thirds of all our planet's fresh water is locked up there in the form of ice in a continent twice the size of Australia. It is the world's highest continent, with more than half of the land over 2,000m (6,560ft) above sea level. The ice on top reaches to 4,200m (14,765ft). Only a few nunataks (for this and other unfamiliar terms see glossary, page 134) show as bare rock above the sheet of ice which covers 99% of the land; only around the coast are there exposed areas where birds and seals may breed. Mean annual precipitation is less than 12cm (4¾in), all falling as snow to perpetuate a polar desert. It is the region of most active glaciation in the world.

This harsh physical environment is plagued with katabatic winds which spring up without warning and roar down glacier valleys at anything up to 200km/h (120mph). The windchill effect can be numbingly serious.

Unlike the Arctic, which is an ocean surrounded by continents, the Antarctic is a continent surrounded by ocean – the Southern Ocean. Between latitudes 40° to 65°S an uninterrupted wind circulates vigorously to develop into the notorious 'roaring forties, furious

THE ANTARCTIC CONVERGENCE

The Antarctic Convergence is the circumpolar region, conveniently drawn as a line undulating between 50° and 60°S, and well defined by thermometer readings – it is sometimes marked by a localised belt of fog or mist – where the warm, more saline surface currents coming south from the tropics meet the cold, denser and mainly non-saline waters moving north from the Antarctic. These conflicting currents clash, converge and sink. The mixing waters provide a sympathetic environment for an abundance of plankton, so the Convergence nourishes huge numbers of seabirds and sea mammals. Note that South Georgia lies south of the Convergence and thus qualifies biologically as an Antarctic Island (unlike the Falklands, for example). This book deals with the wildlife found south of the Antarctic Convergence.

fifties and screaming sixties' – the West Wind Drift. Around the coast there is a contrary circulation in the East Wind Drift. The interaction between these winds and sea currents creates a region of turbulence and as a consequence the Southern Ocean is richly productive, its abundant plant and animal plankton sustaining large numbers of seals and whales, some of which are slowly recovering from exploitation and abuse, as well as many millions of seabirds.

Most Antarctic life clings to the edge, where beaches and cliffs offer snow-free nesting places for birds and pupping places for seals. Much of it is concentrated on the islands – the sub-Antarctic islands and the islands of the Antarctic Peninsula, that last fling of the Andes which extends as a string of islands reaching out into the South Atlantic before swinging round to form a backbone attached to the great Antarctic continent. The backbone is bordered by a necklace of islands which are home to millions of penguins, petrels and seals in the summer season.

Winter is a different story. At the end of March, at the South Pole, the sun sets on six months of icy darkness. As the sea freezes out from the continent's edge at the rate of five kilometres (over three miles) a day, the solid surface doubles. Only Weddell seals and emperor penguins are hardy enough to survive these dark days. Even on the coast the temperature will fall below –40°C. Only the more northern sub-Antarctic islands remain free from sea-ice. Most creatures move north, returning only when the sun shows its face again in the austral spring.

This book reviews the creatures which live south of the Antarctic Convergence. This turbulent area, where the sea temperature suddenly drops by several degrees, nourishes a wealth of tiny sea creatures which in turn support the world's greatest concentration of wildlife. Polar regions lack diversity; there are relatively few species here by comparison with the tropics or the temperate regions. But you may walk all day in a tropical jungle and see precious few animals, whereas at sea in the Southern Ocean or ashore on the islands and the coast of Antarctica there are birds and seals in glorious abundance. What's more, they are unafraid of human visitors. Treat them with respect, move slowly and quietly, and they will tolerate intrusion with equanimity. Better still, sit down quietly and they will come to you in innocent curiosity. It is a magical experience for anyone nurtured in regions where animals long ago learned to fear us.

It is possible to get very close to the animals which live here, but it is important not to overstep the mark. Disturbed penguins make easy prey, and less inhibited birds like skuas or gulls are quick to take advantage of an unguarded egg or chick. Mosses and lichens take a long time to grow in this climate; try not to walk on them unnecessarily.

The IAATO guidelines (see page 136) make a lot of sense; it is vital that visitors to this magical place subscribe to them. And it is important that many of us go there – to enjoy and wonder at the sheer beauty and abundance of the place – because that will produce a body of enlightened ambassadors, our best guarantee that this mighty wilderness will endure.

DISCOVERY AND EXPLOITATION:

EXPLORERS, SEALERS AND WHALERS

The earliest written reference to any penguin was in the account of Vasco da Gama's voyage to India in 1499, in the *Angrade Sao Bras*. In his log he wrote of birds 'as large as ganders and with a cry resembling the braying of asses, which could not fly'. This was off the South African coast and the birds were known then as jackass penguins (African penguins now!). The earliest certain reference to South American penguins was in 1519, on Magellan's expedition in the carrack *Trinidada*. During his circumnavigation he discovered the now-famous Magellan Strait, between Tierra del Fuego and the Patagonian coast. Antonio Pigafetta, an Italian scholar travelling with Magellan, wrote in his journal,

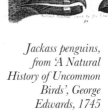

> 'Following the Patagonian coast we found huge flocks of strange geese. On two islands we replenished with penguins and seals, penguins [Magellanic penguins] being all of black colour, and such as cannot flye.'

Jackass penguins, from 'A Natural History of Uncommon Birds', George Edwards, 1745

There is little doubt that the word 'penguin' is derived from the Latin *pinguis*, 'fat', which originally gave the name to the northern great auk. Magellan's sailors, bringing their Portuguese version *pingüim*, would certainly have noted the similarity between this strange version of the northern bird (also of upright posture and flightless, though unrelated).

Penguins were popular with early explorers, partly because of their quaint characters and their human stance, but also because they were available in tightly packed colonies and easy to catch. The fact that they were good to eat was a real bonus of which the men were quick to take advantage.

In December 1577 Francis Drake sailed south from Plymouth in the *Pelican* (later re-named *Golden Hind*).

Until this time, British interests had been more concerned with finding the much-sought Northwest Passage in the high Arctic. But now, as relations with Spain became strained, Drake and Hawkins pioneered south in search of the trade and plunder hitherto claimed as the exclusive rights of the Spaniards. Drake coasted Patagonia and entered the Straits of Magellan, writing in his log (August 1578),

> '...such plenty of birds as is scant credible to report. Great store of strange birds which could not flie at all, nor yet runne so fast as that they could escape us with their lives; in body they are less than a Goose, and bigger than a Mallard, short and thicke sett together, having no feathers, but instead thereof a certaine hard and matted downe; their beakes are not much unlike the bills of Crowes, they lodge and breed upon the land, where making earthes, as the Conies doe, in the ground, they lay their egges and bring up their young; their feeding and provision to live on is in the sea, where they swimm in such sort, as nature may seeme to have granted them no small prerogative in swiftnesse, both to prey upon others, and themselves, to escape from any others that seeke to seize upon them; and such was the infinite resort of these birds to these Ilands, that in the space of day we killed no lesse than 3000.'

Gentoo penguin, from 'Voyage à la Nouvelle Guinée', Pierre Sonnerat, 1776. 'I consider the penguins as amphibious animals, partaking of the nature of birds, beasts and fishes.'

Early mariners were hard put to it to classify these strange animals. They weren't sure whether they were birds, beasts or fish. Pierre Sonnerat, on a French expedition, wrote:

> 'On Pengwin Island there is a fowle so called, that goes upright, his wings without feathers, hanging down like sleeves faced with white: they fly not, but walke in pathes and keep their divisions and quarters orderly; they are a strange fowle, or rather a miscellaneous creature, of Beast, Bird and Fish. They have nothing of the taste of Flesh, and for my part, I take them to be feather'd Fish.'

Feathered fish or not, seafarers regarded a penguin as a penguin as a penguin; it was simply good to eat. Realisation that there were different species came only slowly. Sailors must certainly already have seen chinstraps, macaronis, gentoos and the New Zealand crested penguins, but it was 1758 before Linnaeus, in the tenth edition of *Systema Naturae*, gave the scientific name *Spheniscus demersus* to the African penguin. (Just as well it has one recognised scientific name for in everyday life it has been known variously as the jackass/black-footed/spectacled or cape penguin.)

Captain James Cook. Portrait by Nathaniel Dance, RA (Maritime Museum, Greenwich)

Over the next two centuries 16 other penguin species were recognised. Yet, by the second half of the 18th century, no European had seen the much-conjectured continent of Antarctica. Charts recorded *Terra Australis Incognita* – 'The unknown south land' – and there were any number of dotted islands marked ED (existence doubtful) and PD (position doubtful). Though it is probable that Polynesian canoeists had already been to the far south – their legends refer to the 'frozen ocean' – in European terms it was well into the late 18th century before the Antarctic was discovered.

In July 1768 Captain James Cook set off from Plymouth on the first of two great voyages, expeditions on which he was to be the first to swing about the world in sub-Antarctic latitudes. A great navigator, he was probably the first man to come within sighting distance of the Antarctic continental coast. It was now that the age of primary discoveries began to blossom into the age of scientific exploration. The object of Cook's expedition was astronomical, geographical and biological research. Penguins at last began to take shape as something more than an ingredient for the cook in the galley. Joseph Banks, a scientist on HMS *Resolution*, wrote in his journal for January 7 1769:

Sir Joseph Banks. Portrait by Benjamin West (original in the Usher Gallery, Lincolnshire County Council)

'Blew strong, yet the ship still Laying too, now for the first time saw some of the birds called Penguins by the Southern navigators; they seem much of the size and not unlike *Alca pica* (Razorbill) but are easily known by streaks upon their faces and their remarkably shrill cry different from any sea bird I am acquainted with.

'The sea coast is also frequently visited by many Oceanick birds as Albatrosses, Shearwaters, Pintados,

> &c. and has also Penguins, which are between birds and fishes, as their feathers especially on their wings differ but little from Scales: and their wings themselves, which they use only in diving and by no means in attempting to fly or even accelerate their motion on the surface of the water, might thence almost as properly be called fins.'

On his second voyage, Cook, again with HMS *Resolution* (a Whitby collier of 462 tons), sailed with the object of proving or disproving the existence of a polar continent. On the way he made discoveries in the sub-Antarctic. In 1773 he found the little blue penguin in Dusky Bay, New Zealand and in Tasmania he collected Australian crested penguins. Two years later, penetrating to the deep south in search of *Terra Australis*, he crossed the Antarctic Circle as the first man ever to do so, his farthest latitude being 71°10'. Solid pack-ice blocked his way. He turned back, correctly believing that the ice and land extended to the South Pole. His opinion, pithily expressed, was that no good would come to anyone who persevered further.

King penguins were first described for science when Cook discovered South Georgia in 1775, but confusion was still rife in 1824, when the juveniles were pictured in J A Latham's 'General History of Birds' as a wholly different species, the 'woolly penguin'.

On January 17 1775 he reached South Georgia, taking possession and naming it for King George III. And he promptly took possession also of some king penguins, now described for science for the first time (though the Frenchman Louis de Bougainville had already seen them in the Falklands). However, Cook was not greatly taken by these spectacular islands...

> 'Lands doomed by Nature to perpetual frigidness, never to feel the warmth of the sun's rays, whose horrible and savage aspect I have not words to describe. Such are the lands we have discovered, what then may we expect those to be, which lie still further to the south? For we may reasonably suppose that we have seen the best, as lying most to the North. If anyone should have resolution and perseverance to clear up this point by proceeding farther than I have done, I shall not envy him the honour of the discovery; but I will be bold to say, that the world will not be benefitted by it.'

He was wrong, of course. He was underestimating the commercial value of the fur and elephant seals he had seen in enormous numbers and the determination

Elephant seal. Engraving from Jardine's 'The Naturalist's Library', 1839

of men to seek them out. On returning to Plymouth in 1775, he published an account of his voyage. News of his discoveries and the undreamed wealth of animal life in the Southern Ocean unleashed fleets of sealing expeditions by mariners who had honed their skills in Arctic waters. Trade, in the form of ruthless and indiscriminate slaughter, followed the flag with a vengeance.

The first British sealers reached South Georgia in 1786, killing fur seals at first, then elephant seals for their oily blubber. Americans and a rapid development of the industry soon followed them. By 1791 over 100 vessels were engaged in the seal industry in the Southern Ocean. Vast tonnages of pelts and of oil were taken from South Georgia for the London market.

Fur seals escaped the worst of the carnage until 1792, when Captain Daniel Greene, from New Haven in Connecticut, came to South Georgia in the *Nancy*. He was the first to carry fur seal skins to China, as a speculation. The Chinese market was insatiable. In 1800, in what was probably the most profitable sealing voyage ever made to South Georgia, Captain Edmund Fanning of New York, with the *Aspasia*, took 57,000 fur seal skins and carried them direct to China. At five or six dollars apiece, he made a killing on the Shanghai market. Sixteen other British and American vessels were sealing in South Georgia at the same time, but it was the Americans who monopolised the fur seal trade. British furriers didn't pay enough for the pelts, while the Chinese used them only for making felt.

Captain Fabian Bellingshausen. From 'The Voyage of Captain Bellingshausen to the Antarctic Seas 1819–1821', F Debenham, 1945

When the Russian explorer Bellingshausen, with *Vostok* and *Mirnyi*, reached these latitudes in 1820, there were hardly any fur seals left. (He watched sealers at work, and took a couple of albatrosses and a live parrot from them in exchange for three bottles of rum). Bellingshausen went on to become, arguably, the first man to sight the Antarctic continent on January 27 1820.

Three days after Bellingshausen, but first to sight the Antarctic Peninsula, came Edward Bransfield of the Royal Navy. Captain Nathaniel Palmer, of Stonington, Connecticut, sighted the Antarctic mainland on November 16 1820, having been beaten to it by Bellingshausen, but he went on to become a co-discoverer of the South Orkneys (the South Sandwich Islands had already fallen to Captain Cook in 1775).

In the South Shetlands, the British and Americans were carving up what remained of the fur seal populations. Colonies of Antarctic fur seals were virtually exterminated between 1819 and 1823. In just two years, 320,000 skins were taken, the sealing captains simply pushing ever further south in search of fresh prey.

When the Scot, James Weddell, came south in 1822 with *Jane* and *Beaufoy*, he found dense fogs, fresh gales and continual damp.

Penetrating further south than any man before, Weddell reached 74° latitude in the sea now named after him. On January 16 1823 he was well into pack-ice when he discovered the seal which also bears his name, taking a specimen back to Edinburgh where its description was promptly published as the 'Sea Leopard', inviting real confusion with the leopard seal which had been described from a Falklands specimen by Blainville in 1820.

Captain Weddell took a seal in the South Orkneys which he sent back to the Edinburgh Royal Museum where it was incorrectly identified as a sea-leopard. It was in fact new to science and was subsequently named Weddell in his honour.

In less than 50 years the British and Americans between them took a million and a quarter fur seals, and 20,000 tons of elephant seal oil found a market in London alone. In 100 years the fur seals were almost wiped out, and the elephant seals abandoned as no longer lucrative. Yet by the late 1830s the two truly Antarctic penguins had still to be described for science.

It was at this time that a French expedition commanded by Captain Jules César Dumont d'Urville in the corvette *Astrolabe* visited and surveyed the South Orkneys and the South Shetland Islands. Penetrating further south they reached the Antarctic continent and took possession for France – on January 21 1837 a party landed and planted the tricolour on a rock just off the coast of Adélie Land, which Dumont d'Urville named after his wife. (This sector is still the centre of French research.) At the same time he collected specimens and named the little black and white penguins he found there as Adélie penguins. As it happens he also collected a large egg which was found on an ice floe, but fortunately for the British he didn't recognise its significance and the emperor penguin remained unknown to science. (However, description of the crabeater seal is to his credit, though Bellingshausen had already seen it in 1819–21.)

Capitaine de Vaisseau Jules Dumont d'Urville

Two years later, in 1839, James Clark Ross, in command of a British expedition, with HMS *Erebus* and HMS *Terror* (Captain Francis Crozier), came south under instructions from the Admiralty. His purpose was to make a series of magnetic observations in high southern latitudes for the British Association for the Advancement of Science. In Hobart, Tasmania, Ross heard of Dumont d'Urville's successes and, 'impressed with the feeling that England had always led the way of discovery', he determined to penetrate deeper south. Obstructed by land, he felt his way around and circumnavigated the Antarctic continent. His were the first ships to force a way through the sea which bears his name. He discovered and charted 500 miles of new coast in Victoria Land which he claimed for the Crown at Possession Island on January 12 1841.

In his account of that day Ross wrote,

> 'The ceremony of taking possession of these newly-discovered lands, in the name of our Most Gracious Sovereign, Queen Victoria, was immediately proceeded with; and on planting the flag of our country amidst the hearty cheers of our party, we drank to the health, long life, and happiness of Her Majesty and His Royal Highness Prince Albert. The island was named Possession Island. It is situated in lat. 71°56', and long. 171°7'E., composed entirely of igneous rocks, and only accessible on its western side. We saw not the smallest appearance of vegetation, but inconceivable myriads of penguins completely and densely covered the whole surface of the island, along the ledges of the precipices, and even to the summits of the hills, attacking us

vigorously as we waded through their ranks, and pecking at us with their sharp beaks, disputing possession; which, together with their loud coarse notes, and the insupportable stench from the deep bed of guano, which had been forming for ages, and which may at some period be valuable to the agriculturalists of our Australasian colonies, made us glad to get away again, after having loaded our boats with geological specimens and penguins.'

Possession Island, Victoria Land. From 'A Voyage of Discovery and Research in the Southern and Antarctic Regions during the Years 1839–43', Sir James Clark Ross, 1847: Murray

A year later in latitude 66°S and longitude 156°W, Ross was drifting with the pack-ice, searching for a lead. On the floes were parties of emperor penguins. They had of course been seen before, but now they were collected and formally described for science. In his log he writes:

'During the last few days we saw many of the great penguins, and several of them were caught and brought on board alive. These enormous birds varied in weight from sixty to seventy-five pounds [27–34kg]. The largest was killed by the *Terror's* people, and weighed seventy-eight pounds [35kg]. They are remarkably stupid and allow you to approach them so near as to strike them on the head with a bludgeon, and sometimes, if knocked off the ice into the water, they will almost immediately leap upon it again as if to attack you, but without the smallest means either of offence or defence.

HMS 'Erebus' and 'Terror' pushing through the pack-ice. Emperor penguin in foreground. Ibid.

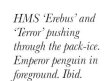

'Some of these were preserved entire in casks of strong pickle, that the physiologist and comparative anatomist might have an opportunity of thoroughly examining the structure of this wonderful creature. Its principal food consists of crustaceous animals; and in its stomach we frequently found from two to ten pounds' [1–4.5kg] weight of pebbles… Its capture afforded great amusement to our people, for when alarmed and endeavouring to escape, it makes its way over deep snow faster than they could follow it: by lying down on its belly and impelling itself by its powerful feet, it slides along upon the surface of the snow at a great pace, steadying itself by extending its finlike wings which alternately touch the ground on the side opposite to the propelling leg … I was in the habit of examining the stomachs of most of the bird which I shot and preserved for the Government

Collection;... In one of these individuals I found upwards of a pound of small fragments of rocks; comprising, basalt, greenstone, porphyry, granite, vesicular lava, quartz, scoriae, and pumice.'

Catching the great penguins, from Ross

Ross waxed lyrical about the scenery,

'...feelings of indescribable delight upon a scene of grandeur and magnificence far beyond anything we had before seen or could have conceived.'

But he foresaw disaster for the seals and whales,

'hitherto beyond the reach of their persecutors, they have enjoyed a life of tranquillity and security; but will now, no doubt, be made to contribute to the wealth of our country, in exact proportion to the energy and perseverance of our merchants; and these we well know, are by no means inconsiderable ... It cannot fail to be abundantly productive.'

Although penguins had been taken in great numbers for food by the early mariners, they were not systematically exploited for their oil until the late 19th century. Penguin eggs, however, are edible, and possibly more important than the flesh as a source of food. They tend to have red yolks, presumably on account of the carotenoid pigment in krill. The sealers stored quantities of eggs between layers of sand after immersing them in seal oil. On one raid alone a rockhopper colony was relieved of 56 barrels of eggs. In 1832 one ship's crew collected 50 barrels of Magellan eggs at Cabo dos Bahias. They used an egg hook consisting of an iron hoop on the end of a pole to extract the egg from deep in the nest burrow.

Penguins have such fine, dense feathers, evenly distributed over their bodies, that the skins have been put to a number of uses in the world of fashion. The Indians of Tierra del Fuego made good use of penguins 'whose Flesh yielded them food, their Skinnes clothing' and made themselves 'a Cloke of Penguin skinnes' according to Hakluyt, who also says: 'These skinnes they compact together with no less industrie and Art than Skinners do with us.'

Even Antarctic explorers and, more recently,

Antarctic scientists, used king penguin skins to prepare fancy slippers.

The thick layer of fat beneath penguin skins, 2cm (¾in) thick in the case of kings, has been eagerly exploited. In 1867 one company is reported to have collected 230 x 500 litres (50,700 gallons) of blubber from 405,600 birds. At 8p a gallon this fetched £4,119, a formidable sum at that time. It was this kind of slaughter which eventually roused naturalists to press for legislation.

Traders boiled king penguins on South Georgia in large quantities for oil. Klutschak, who visited the island in 1877 aboard an American schooner, wrote:

> 'Human greed has been the cause of great persecution of these creatures. I am told that oil made from penguin fat was formerly utilised in tanning leather, and that vessels came for the purpose of taking these birds in huge numbers in order to extract the oil. Proof that they were slaughtered in former times may be seen along the whole northern and northeastern coasts where the small iron trypots, always arranged in pairs, still lie about. At French Harbour parts of a French penguin-hunting ship, which was wrecked in this labyrinth of reefs, may still be seen.'

A trypot used to be the logo of the South Georgia Museum.

In fact the trypots were mostly used for 'trying' elephant seal blubber; penguins were used for fuel.

The most famous of all penguin-oil factories was on the Macquarie Islands. In 1891 Joseph Hatch, a New Zealander, was granted a lease to collect penguin oil. The episode lasted more than 25 years, and was highly successful, but finally succumbed in the face of organised public opposition. At first, Hatch concentrated on the king penguins but found that it was difficult to extract their oil without getting it contaminated with blood, so he turned his attention to the smaller but even more plentiful royal penguins. The season began in February, when the year-old juveniles, or 'fats', came ashore to moult. Later, in March, the adult birds were taken, the season lasting six weeks, in which time something like 150,000 birds were dealt with. But in spite of these numbers, and probably by accident, the arrangement involved the least possible damage to the population, taking place before the breeding season began, and involving only a fraction of the incoming birds. So long as the number taken in a season did not exceed the potential annual increase, the system could, and almost did, continue indefinitely.

The birds were herded into pens, killed and placed in the 'digesters', 900 representing a 'charge'. The dead birds were carried to the upper part of the digester along a railed plank. And it was this part of the process which gave rise to the false story of penguins being driven alive up a ramp until they fell into the boiling vat.

Joseph Burton, who worked on Macquarie for three years as a 'collector' for Mr Hatch, wrote:

> 'The royals are good for the amount of oil they yield when boiled down. Boiling down takes place from January to March. As many as 2,000 birds can be put through the digesters in a day, equal to fourteen casks of oil, each about forty gallons.
>
> 'By placing a fence across their path the penguins, when coming from sea, can be easily driven and yarded like sheep. When the yard is full, ten men go out and club the birds before breakfast. When work is resumed many of the poor birds are found to have recovered and are walking about; they require re-clubbing. The bodies, as they are, are passed into digesters, and boiled by steam for twelve hours. The crude oil is then blown into coolers, casked, and is ready for removal to New Zealand, or elsewhere, for refining.'

Each bird yielded half a litre (one pint) of oil and it fetched £18 per ton. It was of good quality, used for soapmaking and leather dressing.

Joseph Hatch was vilified on all sides. The 'boiling alive' story, widely believed, had the general public and scientific societies howling for his blood. He survived a great deal of organised opposition and litigation, but the final straw to the public came when he claimed that there were more royal penguins on Macquarie than when he had begun operations. No one would swallow this, Hatch was branded a liar as well as a rogue, and the government was finally persuaded to terminate his lease. Scientists have since studied all the available data and come to the conclusion that

Joseph Hatch was telling the truth, and that in fact the rookery was expanding in size during the period of his depredations.

Legal protection for penguins was non-existent until the 19th century, and not until the early 1900s was it begun in earnest. In 1905 the International Ornithological Congress in London passed a resolution urging the governments of Australia and New Zealand to put an end to the destruction of the penguins, which were being boiled for their oil. South Georgia penguins were protected from 1909. In the Falkland Islands, where penguins had enjoyed a measure of protection since 1864, all penguins were protected by 1914. In 1919, the Tasmanian government stopped all licences to exploit penguins on Macquarie Island, which finally became a wildlife sanctuary in 1933. (The French declared the Kerguelen Islands a national park in 1924.)

'Beyond 40° south is no law, Beyond 50° south is no God.' Whalers' saying

Antarctic whaling had a late start. Although Captain Carl Anton Larsen took *Jason* to South Georgia for a reconnaissance expedition in 1892/3, he caught no whales at this time. However, he was well aware of the development of Sven Foyne's deadly harpoon gun. Mounted in the eyes of steam catchers it revolutionised the old-style whaling from open boats associated with sailing vessels. Devastating inroads on the hitherto abundant whale populations began in earnest in 1904.

In 1908 the first control on whaling was promulgated by the Falkland Islands government when it passed the first whaling ordinance, after granting a lease to an Argentine company to process whales at Grytviken in South Georgia in 1906. On Deception Island in the South Shetlands, the Norwegians were granted leases to operate a shore station, which operated from 1912 until 1931. By this time, over-production of whale oil and the financial crisis jointly caused most of the world's whaling fleets to be laid up and the whaling companies sanctioned the principle of agreed quotas. An International Convention for Regulation of Whaling was signed in Geneva in September of that year by 26 nations, but these did not include Argentina, Chile, Russia or Japan, and the outcome was unsatisfactory.

By 1937 the enormous expansion of the pelagic whaling industry led to the International Whaling Conference in London, and the first comprehensive agreement for conservation of whale stocks. This was the delicate beginning of more effective control.

'I am hopeful that Antarctica in its symbolic robe of white will shine forth as a continent of peace, as nations working together there in the cause of science set an example of international co-operation.' Admiral R E Byrd, US Navy, four years before 1961 treaty

The Antarctic Treaty neither endorses nor refutes the claims of the UK, Norway, France, Chile, Argentina, Australia and New Zealand. It seeks to protect Antarctica from exploitation and war and to promote peaceful measures in the interests of all humanity. All have free access, science being seen as the legitimate expression of national interest. Initiated during the International Geophysical Year, it applies to all territories below 60°S. The treaty, signed by 12 nations in 1959, came into force in 1961. Since then others have joined, including Brazil, India and China. A protocol on environmental protection was signed in Madrid in 1996, imposing a 50-year moratorium on mineral extraction.

The concept of the 1959 Antarctic Treaty, whose object is to preserve Antarctica as a region of peace and international co-operation, was therefore long overdue. This fragile agreement, initiated by the Americans under President Eisenhower, aims to protect Antarctica from despoilment and conserve its living resources.

TERRESTRIAL PLANTS AND INSECTS

The greater part of the Antarctic continent is permanently covered by snow and ice. Less than 1% offers a bare surface suitable for colonisation by plants. That small proportion is mainly around the very edge, on the islands and mainland coast, and on inland nunataks. Temperatures are below –25°C in winter and mostly below 0°C in summer over the continental land mass, where conditions are too dry and too severe for plant life.

In the maritime areas, the influence of the sea encourages higher temperatures, reaching 2°C in summer and falling to around –15°C in winter, when there is some rainfall. This milder, wetter climate allows a relative profusion of plants to grow, especially in the peninsula region, with its close relationship with the islands of the Scotia Ridge to South Georgia and Tierra del Fuego.

There are about 300 species of algae, some of them able to flourish on the surface of snow, others associated with the nutrients derived from penguin and other seabird colonies. There are around 200 lichens, 85 mosses, 25 liverworts and, last but not least, two flowering plants.

Lichens and a few mosses are able to colonise the windswept, dry surfaces of bare rock, and are well adapted to survive the harsh variations of climate. In high summer, rockfaces can reach temperatures of 20°C to 30°C; some of them display colourful orange crusts, fertilised by bird droppings. J B Hooker, the botanist who served with the Ross expedition, visited the continent in January 1843, and he noted the abundance of red lichen near the Adélie penguin colonies:

> '…nowhere else in such profusion; a circumstance which may arise from its preference for animal matter; the penguin rookery of Cockburn Island, which taints the air by its effluvium, being, perhaps, peculiarly congenial to the lichen.'

This lichen was subsequently named *Caloplaca hookeri*, in his honour. Bushy tufts of the fruticose (branching) lichen *Usnea*, ageing from youthful pale green to mature dark green to old and dead black, grow on rocks and over the ground. Other lichens encrust moist, coastal rockfaces where they benefit from salt spray, as well as the nitrogen-rich bird faeces. Zones of black species around high water mark give way to colourful splashes of yellow and orange higher above water level. Inland, other lichens grow sparsely on exposed cliffs to as high as 2,500m (8,203ft).

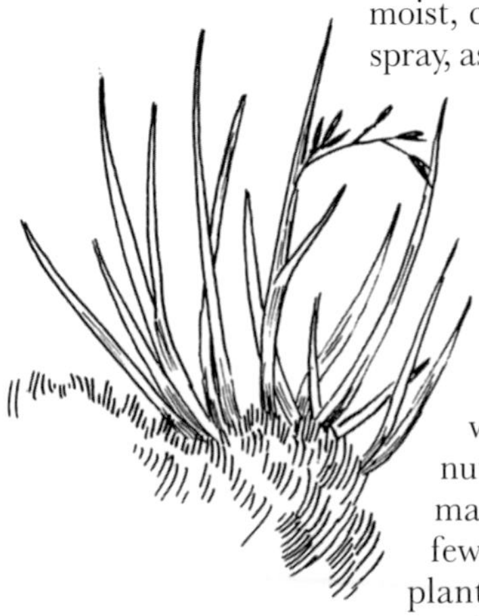

Deschampsia antarctica, Antarctic hairgrass, sheltering by a clump of moss

In high summer, cushions and turves of moss flourish on sandy and gravelly soils, especially where there is some shelter and water. Ponds in the peninsula region derive nutrients from the bird colonies and support mats of blue-green and green algae, as well as a few aquatic mosses. There are only two flowering plants, the Antarctic hairgrass *Deschampsia antarctica*, which occurs in low mats, and the Antarctic pearlwort *Colobanthus quitensis*, which grows in compact cushions. They are found as far south as 68° and are able to tolerate temperatures below zero, at which point they are barely functioning. They are widely distributed, though seldom abundant, in this relatively mild maritime region.

Antarctic midge, Belgica antarctica

In warmer northern lakes, for instance in the South Orkneys, live a few freshwater crustaceans, including a fairy shrimp which reaches 2cm (0.8in), but there are few land insects in the Antarctic. There may be large numbers of tiny land organisms in a few locations, but they are heavily dependent on a supply of water, which means they must live in places which are above freezing point for at least part of the year. The predominant forms are tiny insects (springtails), mites and microscopic protozoans; several species of springtail live in shallow soil, mosses and rock crevices. The largest terrestrial animal, reaching 4mm (0.15in), is a wingless midge, *Belgica antarctica*, which may occasionally be seen crawling over moss on warm sunny days.

MARINE INVERTEBRATES

Antarctic beaches tend to be covered with ice and difficult to get at. But just under the ice there is rich grazing on phytoplankton; tiny sea creatures like copepods, amphipods and mysid shrimps make a living here. Though it may seem an uncomfortable place to be, it has advantages: for instance, the temperature, though low, is constant, and conditions are calm and stable – the ice provides a safe harbour.

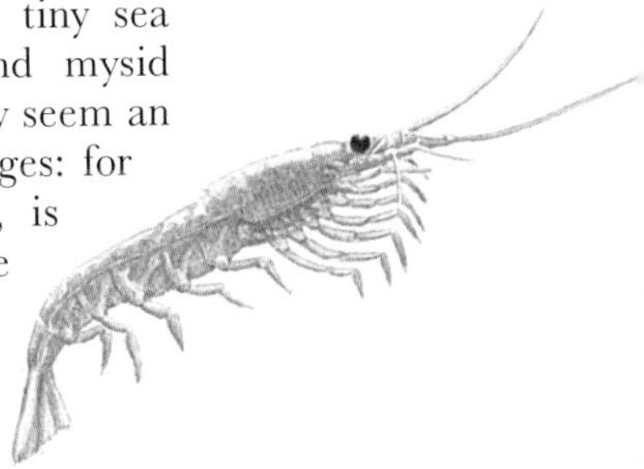

Krill, *Euphausia superba*

Where it is possible to inspect a beach without ice, there will be starfish, soft corals, sea anemones, sea cucumbers and sea urchins in profusion in rocky pool-gardens. One of the common snails will be the Antarctic limpet *Nacella concinna*, which is an important food item for the ubiquitous kelp gulls.

Growth rates depend heavily on season. When days lengthen in early summer and the ice is melting fast, they quicken. In the case of the limpet, it will increase its size by only 0.3mm (0.01in) in a year, something which would be achieved in a couple of weeks in more temperate latitudes. It is a thin-shelled creature, but able to survive even the abrasive force of the pack-ice which scours and scrapes these rocky shores.

It is in the vast Southern Ocean that the majority of Antarctic life finds its nourishment. Mineral upwellings provide the nutrients which are fuelled by the sun to provide life for the astronomical numbers of organisms in the plankton. These floating plants and tiny animals drift more or less passively in the currents, a few to mature into full-grown fish or crustaceans or molluscs or whatever, but most to serve as food for larger predators.

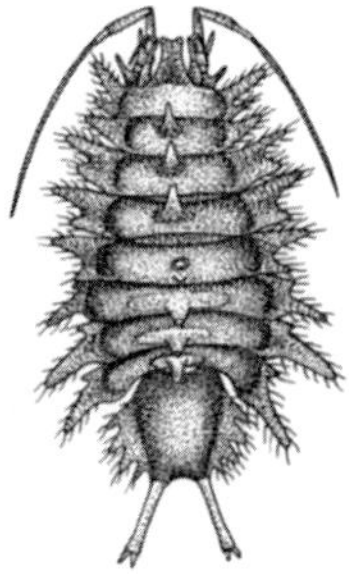

Isopod, *Acanthaspidia may grow to 150mm (6in)*

The shrimp-like krill *Euphausia superba* is the most important of the teeming hordes of plankton animals. Feeding on the phytoplankton, they are themselves the prey of almost all the larger organisms in the sea, from fish to birds to the great whales. They are eaten by almost everything and are the key to the astonishing abundance of Antarctic marine life.

Euphausia superba filters its phytoplankton food by way of a 'filter basket' enclosed by its legs. And it flourishes to swarm in surface waters. Although the individuals may reach no more than a length of 60mm (2½in) they congregate in such numbers that they nourish whales. The swarms may be tens of thousands of metres across, containing animals at densities as high as 10,000 to the square metre. Large swarms may involve several million tonnes of krill, and they move through the sea almost as a single organism, making life easier for the creatures which prey on them.

Krill cooked in the hot volcanic waters around Deception Island

Euphausiid crustaceans are a staple diet for penguins. Five million Adélie penguins on a single island in the South Orkneys have been calculated to need up to 9,000 tonnes of krill and larval fish to nourish their chicks at the height of the season, and this astonishing quantity of food is probably available within a radius of 16km (10 miles). Bernard Stonehouse calculated that a contractor supplying sea food at a comparable rate would need a fleet of 17 medium-sized trawlers and port facilities ten times greater than those of Aberdeen.

In spite of their small size, krill are the whale-feed which provides sustenance for the great whales. Whaling skippers hunted their prey by judging the colour of the sea. Vast acreages of the surface were stained reddish-brown or green with algae but pink when swarms of krill were present, ripe for attracting rorquals, the filter-feeding whales which were the preferred catch.

Krill are, of course, potentially a valuable source of protein for human use, easily collected with large nets. Possibly several million tons could be harvested in a year, representing a significant contribution to the world's food needs. Already they are fished in quantity by Russian, east European and Japanese vessels, which can harvest 100 tonnes a day. The animals may be cooked and peeled, and made into sausage, fish paste or livestock feed. But significant inroads into the krill stocks would undoubtedly involve profound consequences for the native Antarctic stocks of whales, penguins and just about every one of the at-present abundant creatures of the deep south.

Apart from krill, squid are a major presence in the deep Southern Ocean. They, too, take large numbers of krill, but are themselves an important prey item, providing sustenance for penguins, petrels and whales. There are perhaps 400 species worldwide. The 20 or so which live in the Antarctic are found primarily in deep water. Some are small, taken by penguins and petrels, but the giant squid *Architeuthis* reaches up to 8m (26ft) and may weigh 100kg (220lb). These are ferocious predators, preying on large fishes as well as krill, and in turn they are the prey of the great sperm whale.

FISH

Antarctic fish populations are inadequately known and are doubtless vulnerable to ill-regulated commercial exploitation.

Two hundred species of fish have been recorded south of the Antarctic Convergence. Many of them, especially those of the coastal waters, are endemic to the region, occurring nowhere else and adapted to the extreme conditions. They tend to be slow-growing. Five families in the order Notothenioidea make up 75% of the Antarctic fish fauna, four of them found only south of the Convergence, isolated there for millions of years. The Antarctic cod *Notothenia coriiceps* (*neglecta*) is the largest fish in this region, as long as 1.5m (5ft) and with an average weight of over 25kg (55lb), although large specimens may reach 70kg (154lb). They are found in the deep waters of the Ross Sea.

Plunder fish tend to be small, within the 10–30cm (4–12in) range. They are scaleless, with characteristically long barbells on the lower jaw. Most of them live near the bottom on the continental shelf. The Antarctic spiny plunder fish *Harpagifer antarcticus* is found in shallow water round the northern end of the peninsula but is common in tide pools in South Georgia.

The dragon fish are elongate animals up to 50cm (20in) long, with snouts like pike and lacking the first dorsal fin. Most have been caught near the bottom in deep water.

One genus, *Pleurogramma*, includes the Antarctic herring, the only truly pelagic plankton-eating fish.

Antarctic fish have developed extreme adaptations to the near-freezing water. (One species, *Trematomus bernacchii*, actually lives under the fast-ice.) They have glycoproteins – antifreeze proteins – in the blood and body tissues.

One large and predatory group, the ice fish, is unique in having no red blood cells. Lacking the oxygen carried by haemoglobin and myoglobin, they manage because the cold Antarctic water is well oxygenated. The clear blood and pale anaemic flesh of these fish give them their family name; even the gills are cream coloured, in contrast to the red gills of most fish.

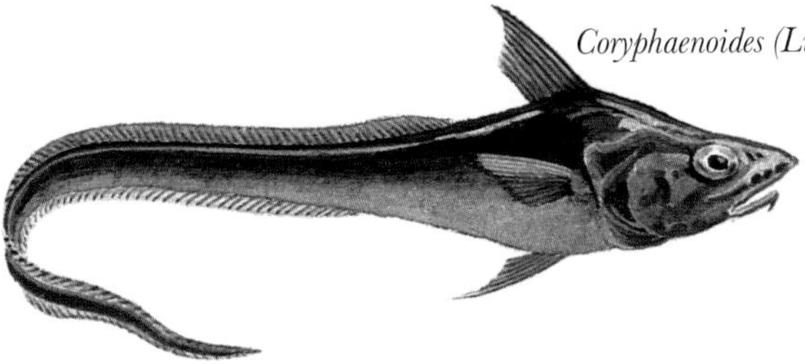

Rat tail
Coryphaenoides (Lionurus) filicauda

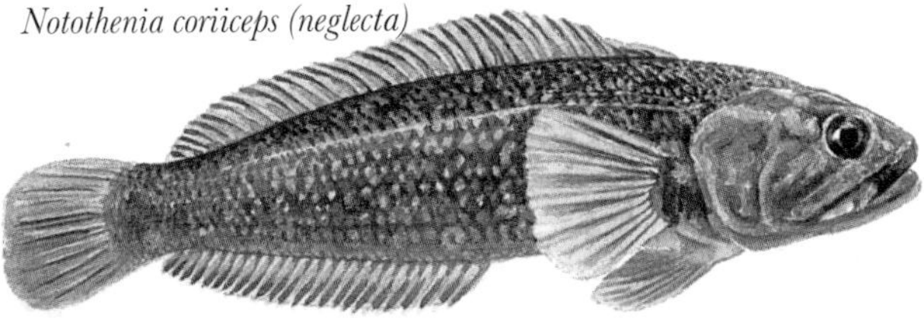

Bullhead Antarctic cod
Notothenia coriiceps (neglecta)

Crocodile dragon fish
Parachaenichthys georgianus

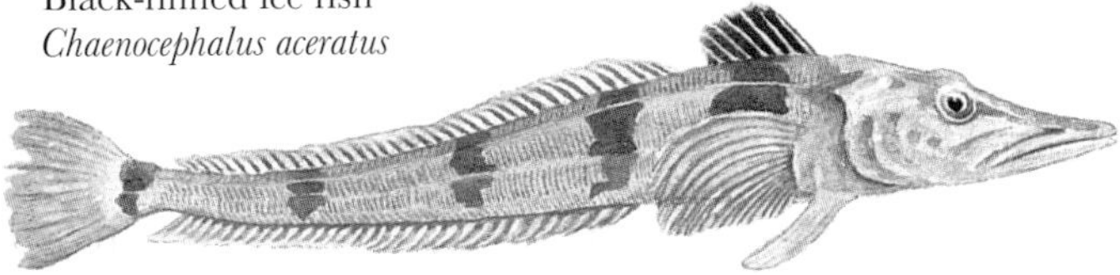

Black-finned ice fish
Chaenocephalus aceratus

Eel pout
Lycenchelys antarcticus

Antarctic spiny
plunder fish
Harpagifer antarcticus

PENGUINS

Penguins have a long history. Millions of years ago, in the Tertiary period, there were at least 25 species in 18 genera. In the Miocene there was a species 1.5m (5ft) tall, weighing well over 90kg (200lb). Today we have 17, some would say 18, species. Contrary to general opinion, few of them live in the Antarctic though they are widespread and virtually confined to the southern hemisphere (the exception being the equatorial Galápagos penguin).

Early explorers thought penguins were fish and classified them accordingly. In fact, as birds, they are superbly designed for their job, flying underwater with great skill. Their compact, streamlined bodies have a deep keel for a breastbone and massive paddle muscles. Their feathers are reduced in size and stiffened, with a fluffy aftershaft at the base. This down creates an insulating layer of air over a thick layer of blubber and skin. Their heads retract to create a perfect hydrodynamic shape. Effectively their bodies are packed in blubber, with a string vest and a windproof outer parka. Their wings are reduced to paddles, and the bones flattened, with the wrist and elbow joints fused, so that although the wing can't be folded, it acts as a powerful propulsion unit. The legs are set well back on the body so that the feet act as control surfaces in the water. Some walk, some progress by jumps, some by tobogganing over ice and snow. Some can climb steep cliff faces, some leap like salmon in order to land on ice floes. On land they walk upright with a seaman's rolling gait. In the water they travel fast by 'porpoising' at the surface or diving

On Scott's first expedition in 1901–1904, Edward Wilson pointed out that nine-tenths of the penguin's distinguishing characteristics appear on the head and neck. Except for size, it would be difficult to identify any of a dozen species if they were found headless. As a consequence of their low freeboard – typical of diving birds – the head is the most conspicuous and significant part of the body in terms of recognition by other penguins.

in pursuit of squids, shrimps or fish. They are highly sociable birds, both at sea and ashore, breeding in colonies which can involve hundreds of thousands of pairs. Those few which breed in tropical or temperate habitats do so underground to avoid the sun. The invisible barrier of warm tropical water denies them access north of the equator. (It is true that the Galápagos penguin breeds just a few miles into the northern hemisphere, but only because the Humboldt current swings around the islands bringing cold water from the Antarctic, forcing the equatorial warm water northwards at that point. Only nit-pickers will deny that the Galápagos penguin is biologically southern.)

Most penguins are enjoying a population increase, possibly as a consequence of over-fishing of baleen whales which has resulted in a super-abundance of krill in the Antarctic. Some, like the macaronis, are in decline for reasons which are not at present fully understood.

Family names of penguin genera

Aptenodytes
wingless diver

Pygoscelis
brush-tailed

Eudyptes
true diver

Megadyptes
big diver

Eudyptula
little true diver

Spheniscus
little wedge

WHY NO WILD PENGUINS IN THE NORTHERN HEMISPHERE?

Penguins cannot tolerate warm sea water. The extreme limit of their range is marked by a line linking places with a mean annual air temperature of 20°C (surface waters are warmed accordingly), so they are effectively trapped by a thermal barrier and restricted to the cold waters of the southern hemisphere.

An ill-fated experiment introduced a small number of king, macaroni and jackass penguins to the Lofoten Islands, off the Norwegian coast, in 1936–38. The last recorded sighting was in 1954. Some suffered at the hands of local people who regarded them as bogeymen. None attempted to nest, probably because there weren't enough of them to encourage the noisy sociability which stimulates courtship. (Penguins breed freely enough in northern zoos, when they are kept in good numbers in close proximity.)

But the experiment was not a good idea anyway. Auks occupy the equivalent niche in northern latitudes and are a hugely successful family, not needing competition from alien penguins. They are not related to penguins, but look alike because they are designed for the same way of life – a classic example of convergent evolution.

KING PENGUIN

Aptenodytes patagonicus

Height
95cm (38in)
Weight
12kg (26lb)

Tall and upright on land, the king penguin has a silvery-grey back with a blackish-brown head decorated with striking orange ear patches. The chicks become woolly-brown as the months go by, and juveniles have pale yellow, auricular patches.

Kings are deep-divers, feeding extensively on lantern fish and medium-sized squid. Over half of their dives, lasting up to eight minutes, take them to a depth exceeding 50m (164ft); the deepest recorded was in excess of 240m (787ft). But it appears that only a small proportion of dives is successful, and much of the time is spent in travelling and searching. They are heavily dependent on the Convergence region for their food. On land they walk slowly and deliberately in a manner which avoids overheating.

Kings are a sub-Antarctic species, but their great stronghold on South Georgia, south of the Convergence, qualifies them for inclusion in this book!

King penguins breed colonially on sub-Antarctic islands in the lower latitudes. Sometimes in huge numbers, they choose raised beaches with easy access to the water and extensive flat or shelving ground, sometimes with tussock. They make no nest but maintain an 'arm's length' territory with vigour.

Their breeding arrangements are highly unusual in that the chick may take more than a year to fledge. The consequence is that king penguins cannot breed annually. Although it is possible for them to breed twice in three years, they mostly breed biennially.

Never far from the colony throughout the year, early breeders – birds which either failed to breed or lost their chicks in the previous year – return in the austral spring for a prenuptial moult, then go to sea for a three-week period of fattening. Courting involves raucous antiphonal calling and displays of the brilliant orange patches in head-flagging. The first eggs are laid in late November, the male standing the first incubation shift of two weeks, holding the large single egg on his feet tucked into the brood patch. The female returns to take the second fortnight shift, after which they alternate for periods of three or four days. The egg hatches in about 54 days, when the parents work shifts of two or three days. By the time it is six weeks old the chick weighs over 7kg (15lb), is half the size and half the weight of its parents and has moulted to a thick brown down coat. It now joins other chicks in a communal crèche, thus allowing both parents to go fishing. By April these chicks are almost full grown, but they will lose weight in surviving the austral winter, to fatten again when food is more readily available in October. In November and December, they moult into juvenile plumage, fledge and go to sea.

If the parents now decide to begin the cycle again, their egg will not be laid until the January/March season and the process will again take well over a year. The result is that at king penguin rookeries there may be birds incubating eggs alongside crèches of 12-month old chicks. The colony is occupied continuously, a consequence of the extraordinarily long breeding cycle in which newly hatched chicks and last year's chicks exist side by side.

After suffering extensive exploitation by man for their oil in the 19th and early 20th centuries, kings are now recovering in numbers. The world population is said to exceed a million pairs.

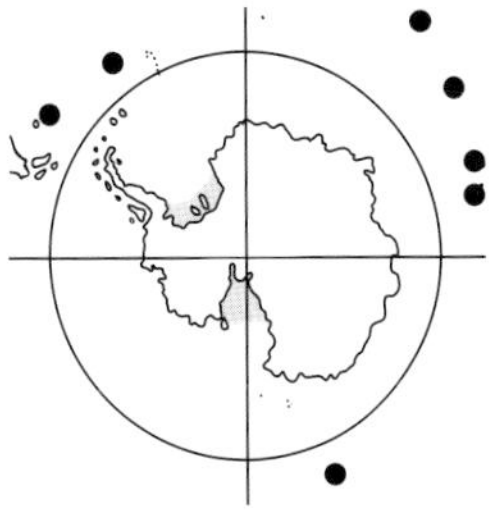

Adult kings are sedentary birds, mainly fishing close to the colony. Some travel as far as South Africa and mainland Australia and New Zealand, but they rarely venture further south into icy seas. Some 100,000 pairs of kings breed on South Georgia, 10% or the world population.

EMPEROR PENGUIN

Aptenodytes forsteri

Height
115cm (42in)
Weight
male 38kg (84lb); female smaller

The sexes are alike, with blue-grey upperparts and blackish-blue heads decorated with large yellow and white ear patches. Underparts are mostly white but the upper breast shows a pale yellow.

Emperors are truly birds of the high Antarctic, seldom seen in sub-Antarctic waters. They are deep-divers, hunting fish and squid in the twilight zone, mostly at about 50m (165ft), but down to as much as 500m (1640ft), well below the summer levels of plankton abundance. Though the proportions vary according to location, generally speaking they take 95% of fish to 3% of squid. The remaining 2% comprises crustaceans, taken by shallow dives under ice-floes. The longest recorded dive was of 22 minutes. On the surface emperors cruise at about 7.5km/h (nearly 5mph).

Emperors breed on sea-ice, in the coldest conditions endured by any bird, and never touch land in their whole lives. The cycle begins in the early austral winter, as soon as the new sea-ice is strong enough to bear their weight. Arriving in March or April, they congregate on fast-ice at the edge of the continental coast and some off-islands. The requirement is for ice which will break up in the following spring. At this time, the adults are fat, weighing up to 10kg (22lb) above their normal weight. Courtship involves much trumpeting, display of their golden flashes and pair bonding. They establish no fixed territory, owning only the ice around them wherever they stand.

The single egg is laid in May/early June, at the onset of the coldest weather, when, uniquely among seabirds, the male takes responsibility for the entire 62–66 days of incubation in the dark Antarctic winter, carrying the egg cradled on his feet, covered by a fold of abdominal skin, and protected from the weather by huddling with the multitude of other male penguins. The female spends the incubation period fattening at sea and returns with a full crop at about the time of the chick's emergence.

Astonishingly, the male, which after its long fast (averaging 115 days) has lost 45% of its bodyweight, gives the naked chick's first feed. It feeds the chick with a secretion of fat and protein from its crop. Now the male bird trudges off to the sea to feed, a journey which may take several days.

The chick soon moults into its first 'Biggles' suit of down. Fed at first by its mother, then alternately by both parents, it joins the crèche at about six weeks of age, fledging in the spring at about five months, when the shortest walk to the maximum food is available. In a hard season, when the sea-ice persists, many chicks die of starvation. But all being well, the newly fledged or nearly fledged juveniles are carried out to sea as the ice breaks into floes. Fully independent, the young must moult to their diving plumage before their ice floe disintegrates, introducing them to the sea to dive for their own fish.

After the breeding season, emperors moult and disperse to surrounding waters, seldom north of the Convergence, though individuals have reached New Zealand and southern South America and juveniles may be more adventurous than previously recorded.

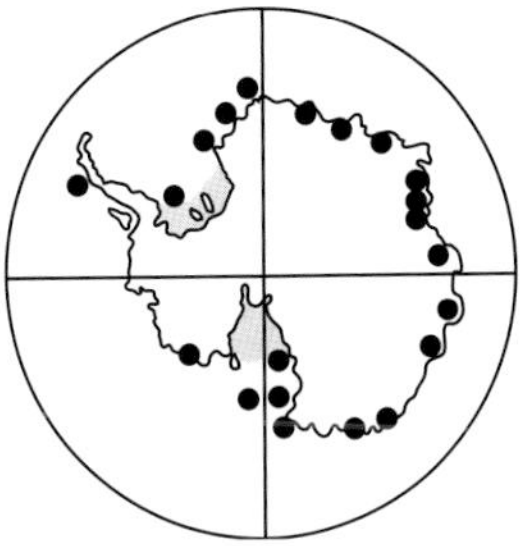

Emperors are sexually mature from about their fourth year, and mostly return to breed in their natal colony. Perhaps a third of the total world population – some 40,000 pairs – breed in the Ross Sea area, but increased exploration is discovering new locations. Other breeding sites are around the Antarctic continent and at the Dion Islands at the southern end of the peninsula.

GENTOO PENGUIN

Pygoscelis papua

Height
76–81cm (30–32in)
Weight
5.5–6kg (12–13lb)

Gentoos become smaller the further south they live. Their slaty-black heads are topped eye to eye with a neat white bonnet, and they have a bright reddish-orange bill. Long, stiff tail feathers stick out behind as they walk, often cocked up in the water. No other penguin has such a prominent tail (*Pygoscelis* means brush-tailed, from the sweeping action).

Gentoos enjoy a varied diet of fish and crustaceans, taken by pursuit in dives which may be in shallow waters for krill or over 100m (328ft) down for fish. Most dives last only half a minute. In northern waters they take mostly fish and half as many crustaceans; at the southern end of their range the mix is 85% crustaceans and 15% fish.

Gentoos return to their colonial breeding grounds, flat areas on rocky coasts (with easy access to the sea by way of a shelving beach) in June/July at the northern end of their range, October/November at the southern end in the peninsula. They are markedly less colonial than other penguins, often in small numbers, often in association with other species. Their attachment to the nest-site is not strong, since they usually nest in places where there is no shortage of possibilities, but their pair-bond is strong, and they usually mate with the partner of the previous season. Rookeries in the north are often on mounds in the tussock or on low hilltops; in the south they are on open beaches, from the shoreline to as high as 50m (161ft), even on fairly steep ridges.

In South Georgia, the nest may consist of grass, leaves, twigs or pebbles; further south it is mainly stones and some odds and ends in a saucer shape, perhaps just a scrape. The nest space is hotly defended. Two eggs are the normal clutch, but usually only one chick survives to fledge. Unlike most other penguins, northern gentoos will replace a lost clutch.

Parents share an incubation period of 31–39 days, and then the chicks are fed on undigested shrimps or small fish by regurgitation. They gather in the protection of crèches at four to five weeks (allowing both adults to go fishing) and fledge at 85–117 days in the north, 62–82 days in the south. Uniquely among penguins, the young continue to be fed for a further period by their parents after fledging, so that they are hanging around the moulting area together well into March

The total population of gentoos is somewhere between 300,000 and 350,000, most living south of the Antarctic Convergence, mainly on South Georgia. On land their main predators are Antarctic skuas, though snowy sheathbills take some eggs and chicks. At sea, the danger comes from leopard seals.

On dispersal, the southern birds move away from the winter ice while the more northern population is sedentary, working inshore waters for krill. Adolescent birds are more adventurous, sometimes turning up in New Zealand, South America and South Africa. They are sexually mature at two years of age, but may not find opportunities to breed for several years.

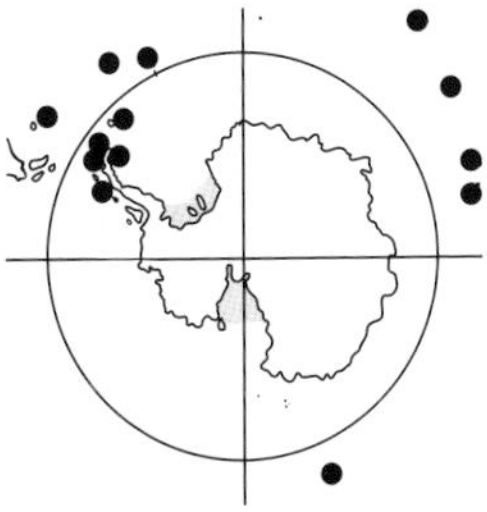

Where does the name come from?
It is said that expat Brits used the term 'gentoo' to describe members of a Hindu sect where the members wore a white cotton cap. But if this is true, how and when did the name reach the gentoos of the far southern hemisphere?

ADÉLIE PENGUIN

Pygoscelis adeliae

Height
75cm (30in)
Weight
5kg (11lb)

Adélies, and a part of mainland Antarctica, were both named after his wife by the French explorer Dumont d'Urville who first described the species for science while planting the French flag on the coast of Adélie Land in 1837 – still the centre of French Antarctic research.

Along with the emperor, the Adélie is the only other truly Antarctic penguin. It breeds further south than any penguin.

The body and head are blue-black, the bill is reddish with a black tip, and the eye is ringed in white. The classic 'little man in evening dress', the Adélie walks well on ice or snow, tobogganing when it chooses. At sea, its cruising speed is 7.2km/h (4½mph). Adélies cluster in huge colonies all around the Antarctic continent, fishing for krill – mainly *Euphausia crystallorophias* in the shelf waters around the continental edge and *E. superba* in peninsular waters.

The maximum recorded fishing dive was to 175m (574ft), but most food is probably caught in surface waters. Of the total catch, 68% is crustacean, the rest fish and cephalopods (though mostly krill along the peninsula).

On their continental breeding grounds, Adélies experience the coldest Antarctic conditions and enjoy the shortest summers. The whole breeding cycle has to be fitted into the few weeks when temperatures rise above freezing and when food is abundant in open water not too far away. The typically dense colonies are established on the ice-free slopes of rocky coasts, headlands and islands, on high ground, often far from open water but offering a practicable route to the sea. The critical requirement is that there should be open water within a few miles in the January/February period when chicks need regular supplies of food.

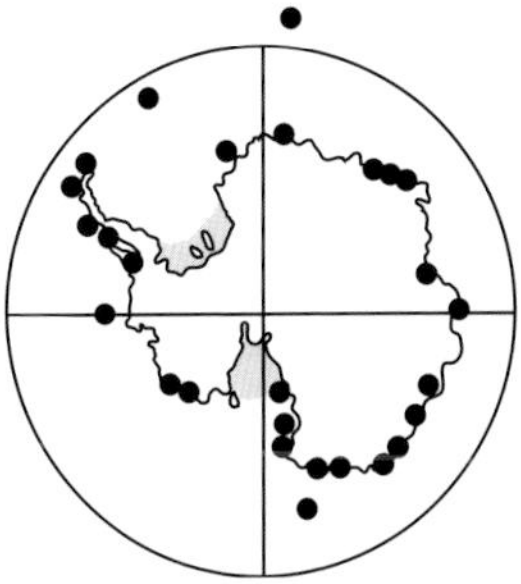

Males are first to return to the breeding grounds, sometimes crossing as much as 60 miles of fast-ice to reach them. The females follow, to join a known mate, but the pair-bond is less strong than in other Pygoscelids: the harsh requirements of the short season allow for no delay. The imperative is to begin courtship, and the male will bond quickly with an available female rather than delay in waiting for last year's mate. Courtship is brief, with much flipper waving and guttural gossip.

The nest is composed of small pebbles in a shallow depression, gathered by stealth and thievery, and jealously guarded because it is vital that the eggs are raised above the level of melt water. Two eggs are laid in mid-November, then incubated for 32–37 days. Hatching in late December, the young are closely attended by a parent till they join the crèche in their third week. Fledging takes 41–64 days, and by mid-February the young birds are at sea, at the time when krill is most abundant. The adult birds abandon the nearly fledged chicks when they are about seven weeks old, then moult either ashore or on an ice floe as it drifts north to the richest feeding waters. The adolescent birds remain in the pack for several years before returning to the natal colony.

Adélie chicks in moult
The silvery-grey baby down is moulted away by the tenth day to be succeeded by a darker grey. Once in the crèche the diving suit begins to appear – first from under the flippers, then another ten days reveals most of the fully formed suit. In five more days the last fluff around the head is lost.

Mortality may be heavy at the colony. On average only 62% of chicks reach the crèche stage, but once they reach the sea they are relatively safe. If they survive the first two or three years they may live to 10 or 12.

Adélies are the most abundant of all penguins, the colonies involving many thousands of pairs and the total population being somewhere in the region of two and a half million pairs, half of them in the Ross Sea area. They are vulnerable to disturbance from scientists and tourists, but adverse weather conditions are their worst enemy. Snow falling on downy chicks may melt and cause death from chilling. Long-term global warming may be responsible for the current population decline.

CHINSTRAP PENGUIN

(Bearded penguin, ringed penguin)
Pygoscelis antarctica

Height
68–77cm (27–30in)
Weight
4kg (9lb)

Smaller and more slender than gentoos or Adélies, chinstraps have blue-black backs with white cheeks and white underparts. A thin black line – the 'chinstrap' – crosses the chin and runs back under the eye to join the nape. Occasionally, the odd leucistic individual appears amongst the multitudes. In the water it often cocks its tail.

The chinstrap's cruising speed is 5km/h (3mph). Food is almost entirely crustacean, with krill taken in pursuit-diving. Although the maximum recorded depth of a chinstrap is 70m (230ft), many dives are inside the 10m (33ft) zone and last for just half a minute.

Chinstraps mainly inhabit islands of the Scotia Arc, concentrating in vast colonies on the coasts of the South Orkneys, South Shetlands and South Sandwich Islands. They are mini-mountaineers, choosing rocky and ice-free slopes, sometimes in association with, but above, gentoos and Adélies, from just above sea-level to as high as 100m (330ft). Male chinstraps are pugnacious creatures, perfectly capable of bullying an

Adélie off its nest in a takeover. They may nest in congregations of many thousands.

Chinstraps are the last of the brush-tailed penguins to return to the breeding slopes, arriving in late October/early November. The first birds occupy the highest places – the first to become ice-free – often on rocky and seemingly inaccessible sites. Using beak and sharp claws they heave and push their way up, sometimes on all fours. Coming down they may toboggan. Unlike the more southerly Adélies they can enjoy a longer breeding period and have a more relaxed attitude. With both a strong attachment to the traditional nest site and a strong pair-bond, the male, arriving first, will wait for his known mate, so there is a tendency for the season to be prolonged.

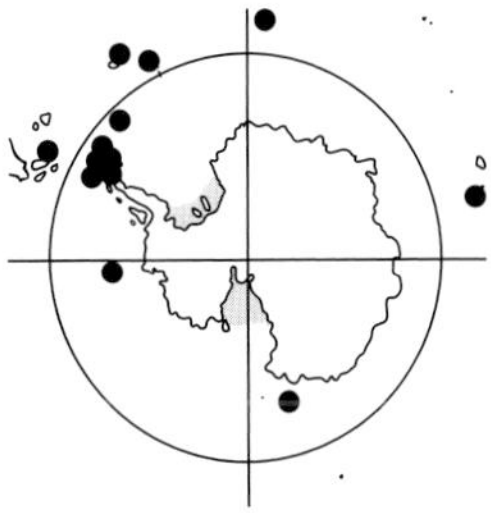

Chinstraps regularly shed the linings of their stomachs, throwing up a yellowy-orange 'burst-balloon', possibly as a response to the accumulation of fluoride contained in their diet of krill.

Like gentoos and Adélies, chinstraps are noisy and sociable. Their courtship is brief, but involves much head-waving and squawking. The nest is an unlined flat saucer of small stones, sometimes decorated with a few bones or feathers. It is most carefully guarded, since neighbours will steal stones if given the least chance. The normal clutch of two eggs is laid from late November through till late December, in a manner possibly less synchronous than the other Pygoscelids. Both parents share the incubation period of 35–38 days. The chicks are fattened on regurgitated krill and join the crèche after the first month or so. Fledged in 52–60 days, they go to sea while the adults begin their moult. It may be well into April and even May before the last stragglers go to sea.

Chinstraps are increasing in numbers, possibly fuelled by the abundance of krill made available because of the scarcity of plankton-feeding whales. The total world population is probably well over seven million pairs.

ODD MAN OUT!

The occasional coffee-coloured (Isabelline) penguin may be seen amongst the hordes of chinstrap or other penguins. These leucistic penguins are not a different species, but the result of a dilution of normal pigmentation. Very rarely an albino occurs.

ROCKHOPPER PENGUIN

(Moseley's penguin)
Eudyptes chrysocome

Height
55cm (21½in)
Weight
2.5kg (5½lb)

The underparts are mostly white, the upperparts blue-black. The back of the head has a black crest and there is a thin but vivid lemon-yellow crest running back from above the eyes (not joining at the forehead), ending in moderately droopy plumes. The eyes are bright red and the bill pinkish-black. The sexes are similar, but the males larger and with heavier bills. Rockhoppers are the smallest polar penguins, weighing only 2.5kg (5.5lb), as against the emperor's 30kg (98lb)! A deep-sea penguin, it dives mainly for krill and amphipods, and possibly small fish and squid.

Rockhoppers are a wide-ranging species with an unusual (for penguins) tolerance of temperature, since members of the three subspecies breed from Tristan da Cunha to just south of the Convergence on Kerguelen, Macdonald and Heard Islands. Most breed north of the Antarctic Convergence (there is a large population on the Falkland Islands, for instance).

E. c. chrysocome is the subspecies breeding below the Convergence, seldom as far south as the pack-ice and not in large numbers. Occasionally an individual appears in the northernmost of the South Shetlands.

True to their name, rockhoppers choose to breed amongst rocks on rocky ground, scree slopes, rocky shores and lava flows close to the sea. The approach to the colonies is very often through heavy surf and involves leaping out on to exposed rocks. They return to the breeding grounds from October, when the males claim the same site as the previous year. The nest will consist of small stones, possibly decorated with a bit of grass or bleached bones. A normal clutch is of two eggs, one being half as big again as the other. The parents share the 34 days of incubation, but almost invariably the smaller egg is lost or fails to hatch: very few of the small eggs result in chicks. At first the male guards the chick while the female goes fishing, then the chick joins a crèche when it is reaching three weeks of age, from which time both parents bring back its krill soup. The chick reaches adult weight and fledges at about ten weeks, when it goes to sea in February/March. The adults precede it to sea to fatten up, then return to the colony for four or five weeks in order to moult, before returning to sea in April/May for the winter. The species is in serious decline for reasons which are not yet entirely clear. Oil pollution and the relatively recent heavy fishing pressure north of the Convergence may be significant.

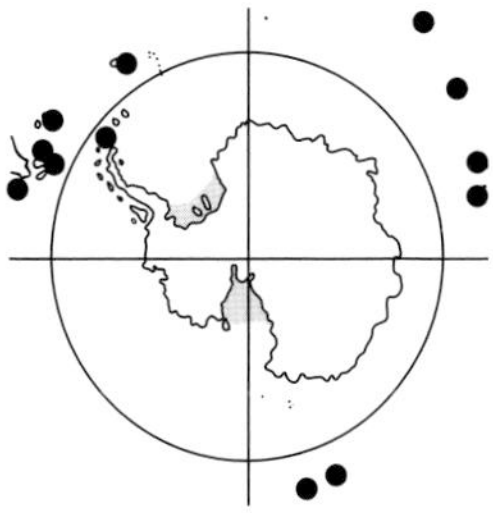

CRÈCHE

As they grow, young penguins gather in large numbers to form communal nurseries or 'crèches' as a form of protection against predators. There is no overall 'nanny' in charge, although if danger threatens the chicks may congregate around an adult bird to help ward off attack. Each chick is fed by its own parents, which recognise their offspring both by calls and by appearance.

MACARONI PENGUIN

Eudyptes chrysolophus

Note the small egg, which has been rejected

Height
70cm (27½in)
Weight
4kg (9lb)

Larger than a rockhopper, with a more robust bill and lacking the black occipital crest, the macaroni penguin has a golden crest which is joined in a broad band across the forehead, extending back over the reddish-brown eyes and sweeping into splendidly drooping plumes.

Macaroni penguins pursuit-dive mainly for krill and squid, and some fish, working mostly in the top 20m (65ft), but sometimes down to a depth of 80m (262ft).

They breed mainly through the Scotia Arc; they are abundant on South Georgia, where there may be more than five million pairs, and they reach the South Shetlands in very small numbers as far south as Livingstone Island.

Macaronis return to the colonies in October, males first, repairing their meagre nest sites with small pebbles. The females follow, and courtship involves much hoarse braying and shaking of the golden plumes. Two eggs are laid and, as in the case of the rockhopper, one is much smaller than the other and is likely to be ejected from the nest. Incubation is for approximately 35 days and by both sexes, which relieve each other for fishing expeditions, organising their shifts so that the female returns with a full crop as the chick is about to hatch. The smaller chick, if it reaches the hatching stage, is of course less likely to survive unless the season is particularly kind to it, but having only one chick to rear probably makes life just possible in the far south for macaronis, which are the least adapted of polar penguins.

The males attend the chick closely for the first three weeks while the female is fishing and returning with a full crop at intervals which depend on the availability of krill – maybe a few hours or a couple of days. The chick or chicks crèche soon afterwards, before they are a month old. They are fed by both parents, and fledge at two months in February or March, when they go to sea as independents. Yearling birds, with grey chins and unsubstantial yellow crests, will be with the colony in December/January and moult to fully adult plumage in February. Post-breeding adults moult in March. By late April the breeding grounds are virtually deserted. The winter months are probably spent at sea in warmer waters further north.

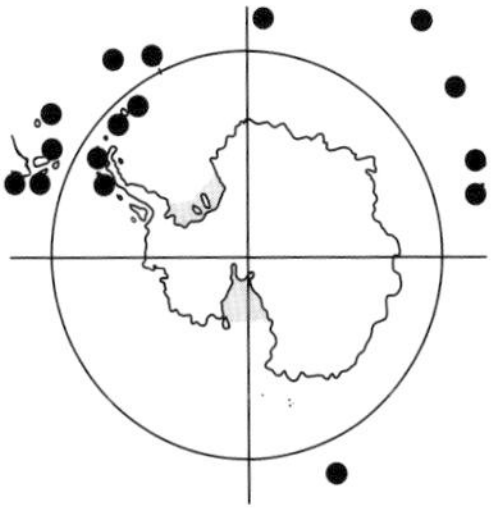

Macaronis are the most abundant of the southern penguins, but their stronghold is in the sub-Antarctic islands where their numbers may reach 12 million breeding pairs. The main concentrations are on South Georgia, Crozet and Kerguelen islands.

Dagwood, in the Blondie cartoon, sports a classic 'macaroni'.

The name 'macaroni' derives from the 18th century dandies who made the Grand Tour to Italy and affected continental tastes and fashions, dyeing their hair in streaks and extending crests over their ears. Arriving back in England they were promptly called 'macaronis' by the yokels, whose only association with Italy was the pasta with which they were familiar. Hence, on the American side of the Atlantic, 'Yankee-doodle went to town, riding on a pony, stuck a feather in his cap and called it macaroni!' On exploring south, both British and US sailors, meeting the gaudily crested penguins, promptly christened them after the hairstyle.

ALBATROSSES

The name is an English sailors' corruption of the Portuguese *alcatraz* for a pelican, a bird which early explorers would have known from the Mediterranean. Albatrosses are divided into two genera, *Diomedea* and *Phoebetria*, but in common language the 14 species are crudely divided into the 'great albatrosses', the wandering and royal; and the 'small albatrosses', collectively better known to seafarers as mollymawks, from the Dutch *mal*, foolish, and *mok*, gull. Another term for them is 'gooney', from the English dialect word for simpleton. These pejorative and richly undeserved epithets were the result partly of seeing albatrosses ashore, out of their element, appearing clumsy, and partly because of their endearing but ill-advised innocence in standing quietly while being bludgeoned by a club and picked up for the pot.

Black-browed albatross, from 'A Natural History of Uncommon Birds', George Edwards, 1745

In the late 18th and 19th centuries albatrosses were much persecuted both for their meat and their plumage, and were also taken in significant numbers on hook and line by sailors who made pouches out of their webbed feet, feather rugs from their skins and pipe stems from their bones.

Albatrosses have stout bodies with large heads on long necks, mostly short tails and strikingly long and narrow wings (over 3.6m (12ft) in the wanderer).

Albatrosses are legendary birds; partly because of their great size but also because they inhabit such remote and storm-ridden seas. Early 17th–century mariners respected their grace and majesty in flight and generally disapproved of killing them at a time when most birds were valued only for their palatability. They also believed that the souls of drowned sailors were reincarnated in albatrosses, increasing the fear that killing them would bring bad luck. However, more recently the breeding colonies were much reduced by the depredations of plumehunters. Under protection, they have recovered, but new threats include drowning in gill-nets, hooking on longlines and choking on floating plastic rubbish.

They have short legs, placed well back, but the most eye-catching feature is the massive hooked bill, covered with a number of horny plates. Adult great albatrosses are mainly white, while the twelve smaller species (mollymawks) have variable quantities of black on the back as well as on the wings. Most are inhabitants of the southern oceans, mainly between 30° and 60°S, but one is based on the equatorial Galápagos Islands, ranging the Humboldt current area. Three are confined to the North Pacific, effectively isolated from their southern cousins by the windless region of the doldrums. None breed on the Antarctic continent.

One authoritative estimate (Bonner 1985) is that there used to be three quarters of a million breeding pairs of albatrosses in the Southern Ocean, which debunks the popular notion that it was teeming with millions. Albatrosses are particularly vulnerable to bycatch on the fishing industries' longlines, when they take the squid used on the baited hooks, and are currently in serious decline.

Albatrosses spend most of their lives in flight, gliding the waves and circling the major wind systems. They are highly accomplished dynamic soarers, seemingly motionless yet totally in control, but they rely on a constant supply of wind and are highly inefficient in flapping flight. In the occasional calm they are forced to sit it out on the surface and wait.

Their food is mainly squid, taken by surface-seizing when they settle on the water, floating high with plenty of freeboard, wings often raised to keep them dry. They will also examine floating weed in the hope of finding fish eggs and they will follow ships for galley waste.

'I now belong to a higher cult of mortals, for I have seen the albatross.'
Robert Cushman Murphy,
October 28 1912, aboard the whaling brig 'Daisy'

They are slow to mature, mollymawks breeding in their sixth or seventh year, great albatrosses in their ninth. Giving evidence of their southern origins, even the North Pacific species breed at the time of the southern summer, October to April. They all breed colonially, on remote oceanic islands. Mating for life, they court with dances which may seem somewhat ungainly to us, bowing and scraping, bill rubbing and wing stretching. The nest is a scrape on the ground or a mud mound lined with a few feathers or grasses. The single chick is fed by regurgitation of stomach oil. The process is long drawn out: from egg-laying to fledging takes a year in the case of the great albatrosses, and as a consequence they breed only in alternate years. Mortality is very high in the first year, but those which survive enjoy long lives, many reaching ages well over 50.

WANDERING ALBATROSS

Diomedea exulans

Length
107–135cm
(42–53in)

Wingspan
254–363cm
(100–142½in)

The plumage of the wandering albatross varies greatly through the years. The first-year bird is dark brown, but as the years go by the body and upper wings become progressively whiter until in old age the male reaches the 'snowy' stage, almost completely white. The underwing pattern remains constant – white with a black rim. Most birds retain dark tips and sides on the tail. As in all albatrosses the hooked pinkish bill is large and involves several horny plates.

These are the world's largest flying birds, weighing over 9kg (20lb), spending adult life riding the prevailing westerlies in the 'furious fifties' and the 'roaring forties' – the west wind drift, circumnavigating the Southern Ocean and coming ashore only to breed.

They are master gliders, with a majestic soaring flight on stiffly outstretched wings. In calm weather or when performing figures-of-eight or ellipses round a ship they sometimes flap slowly. They take advantage of the different wind speeds at different altitudes, heading into the wind to gain height, turning to glide downwind towards the trough between two waves, gaining speed but losing height slowly before turning into the wind to achieve lift again on the upcurrent. In a calm they are unable to fly and must settle on the sea. They are enthusiastic ship-followers, often keeping company for days on end.

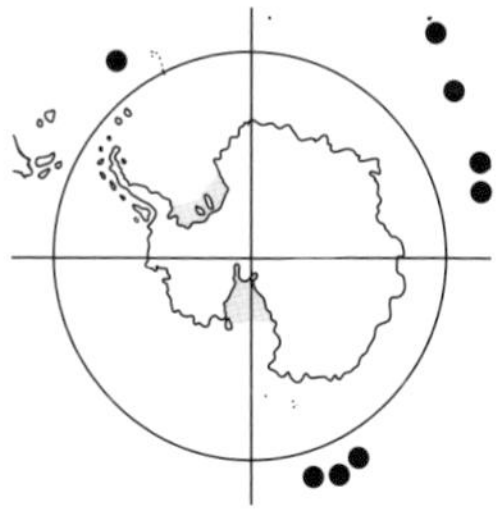

Over 4,000 pairs of wanderers used to breed on South Georgia, with others on Kerguelen and other sub-Antarctic islands. The total world population used to be in the order of some 37,000 pairs, but when they disperse to wander the open sea, they fall foul of the longlining industry which is making serious efforts to solve the problem. The current population is probably in the order of 28,000 mature individuals. *(see box on page 51).*

Wanderers rely heavily on squid, taken by surface-seizing, but they also take fish by surface-seizing and sometimes by shallow plunging. They will poke about in floating seaweed for fish eggs and crustaceans; they search out carrion by smell. In the whaling days they attended whale carcasses for the blubber; nowadays they follow trawlers for offal, other ships for galley waste.

Wanderers patronise remote and windswept islands, gathering in loose colonies on slopes which offer an unimpeded runway for take-off. As large birds, they lay large single eggs which produce chicks needing a long period of growth to fledging. The result is that they breed only in alternate years, and they do not begin breeding till they are probably over ten years of age. Returning to the breeding place in November, they repair and improve the nest – a piled cone of mud and grasses, which is well spaced from the neighbours. Courtship is highly ritualised with much head-waving and spread wings: albatrosses generally pair for life. Both sexes share the incubation period of 78 days in shifts of about ten days. The chicks are fed on a rich mix of partly digested fish, squid and stomach oil.

For the first few weeks the chick is brooded, given constant attention and fed daily, but after that both parents forage, returning at intervals. Fledging takes nine months. Unlike smaller petrels, the newly fledged birds are not abandoned by their parents before they go to sea.

ROYAL ALBATROSS

Diomedea epomophora

Length
107–122cm
(42–48in)
Wingspan
305–351cm
(120–138in)

The adult's head and body are white, the upperwing mostly brown-black with an area of white at the leading edge, the underwing white with black tips to the primaries. The long bill is pale pink to horn-coloured, with diagnostic black cutting edges to the upper mandible, easily seen at close range. In the first stage of plumage the juvenile has a narrow black tip to the tail but subsequently the tail is entirely white.

A master glider, as the wanderer, the royal albatross is less inclined to follow ships, but it will still patronise trawlers. Although firmly based in the New Zealand area, royals nevertheless roam the Southern Ocean, and are not uncommon among the wanderers in the Drake Passage, for instance – look closely at their tails for identification. They feed mainly on squid, as well as fish and some crustaceans, and are often in company with other petrels.

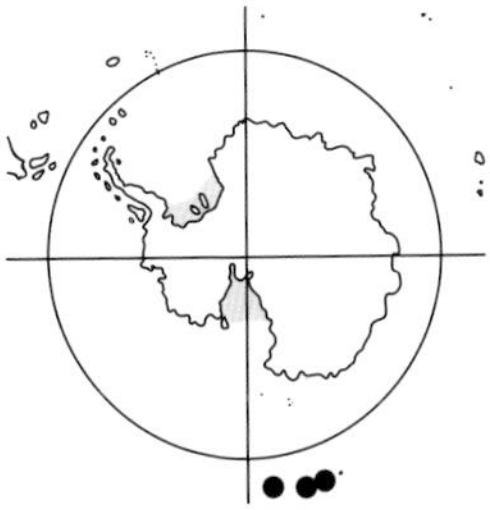

The royal albatross breeds biennially on remote islands around New Zealand. (Most unusually for an albatross, also on the mainland of South Island at Dunedin.) While they are fertile at the age of about five, they breed from about nine years old. They return to the tussocky slopes in October for the ritual bowing, scraping, bill-clacking and wing-raising of courtship, which may also take place on the water. Mating for life, the royal courtship formalities are less prolonged as the years go by. A single egg is laid in November, then incubated for about 79 days by both parents on two to three week shifts. The white downy chick is brooded for over a month and fledges at about 240 days, going to sea in the September or October of the year following its laying. They have long lives: one individual last bred at the age of at least 61.

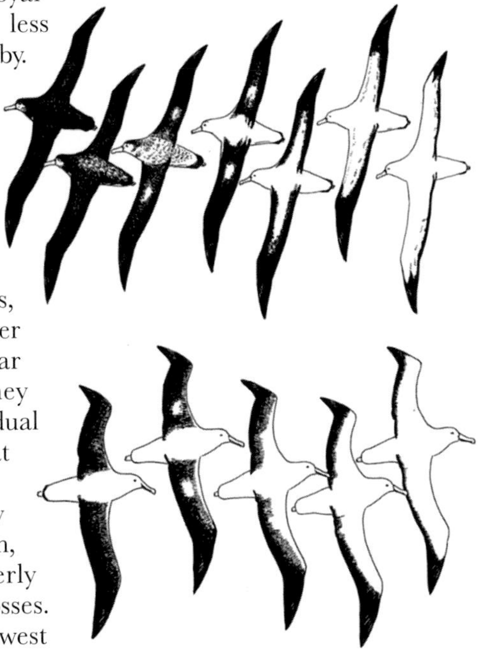

Plumage stages of the wandering albatross (above) and royal albatross (below). After Peter Harrison

Royals disperse widely over the Southern Ocean, circulating in a westerly direction as other albatrosses. Many winter in the southwest Atlantic, some off the coasts of South America and Australia. The total world population may be anything up to 17,000, the main centres being Chatham and Campbell Islands. After over-exploitation on Enderby Island, they are now increasing.

BLACK-BROWED ALBATROSS

(Black-browed mollymawk)
Thalassarche melanophrys

Length 83–93cm (33–37 in)
Wingspan averages 240cm (95in)

The adult bird has a white head with a dark eyebrow smudge which passes through the eye and a bright yellow-orange bill. The upperparts are dark grey, merging into blackish-grey towards the back, and a white rump; underparts are white. The upperwing is entirely brownish-black except for white tips to the primaries. On the underwing dark ends and edges enclose white scapulars. Juveniles are as adults, but are darker under the wing with a dark bill, grey nape and collar.

Circumpolar, widely distributed, common and an enthusiastic ship-follower, the black-browed albatross is sometimes found many hundreds of miles from land, yet it is more common in inshore waters than other albatrosses, even penetrating fjords and harbours, especially in foul weather. Its flight pattern is typical of all albatrosses. It takes its krill and fish prey mainly by surface-seizing, but also by active plunging and diving at the surface, and it will follow trawlers for offal.

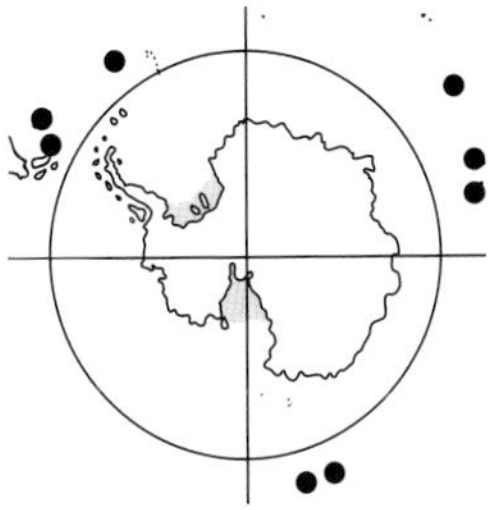

The birds return to the remote sub-Antarctic islands to breed in September or October, sometimes in a mixed colony with grey-headed albatrosses. The substantial nest-cone is of mud and grass, on a steep tussocky slope in close company with others. The single egg is incubated for about 68 days. The chick is brooded for up to four weeks and fledges at about 120 days. It is fed mainly on semi-digested krill and squid by regurgitation. Since the breeding cycle is so much shorter than that of the great albatrosses, the black-browed is comfortably able to breed annually.

Dispersal is generally to the north: black-browed albatrosses commonly reach to 10°S off Peru and 20°S off South Africa, working the cold-water Humboldt and Benguela currents. This northward tendency may account for the regular appearance of this albatross in the northern hemisphere, though it is highly likely that some of them, having been caught on lines by fishermen, are 'helped' through the doldrums and released when they are no longer a novelty. Traditionally fishermen have used them as bait or cosseted them as temporary pets. They are the most abundant and widespread of all albatrosses, with a total world population of over a million, but they are in serious decline.

LONGLINE FISHING

Every year longline fishing vessels, many of them 'pirates', unwittingly drown tens of thousands of albatrosses when they seize baited hooks intended for fish. This has caused a catastrophic decline in albatross populations, threatening the existence of some species. The organisation BirdLife International is aiming to stop the needless slaughter of these magnificent birds by ensuring, in collaboration with the fishing industry, that relevant international agreements are implemented that will benefit both the birds and legal fishing. To support their work, which is already showing real progress, contact http://savethealbatross.birdlife.org.

GREY-HEADED ALBATROSS

(Grey-headed mollymawk)
Thalassarche chrysostoma

Length
81cm (32in)
Wingspan averages
220cm (87in)

Not surprisingly, this albatross has a grey head, with a black bill ridged top and bottom with yellow, and tipped red-orange. The grey of the head and neck merges into a dark back and a dark grey tail; the underbody is white. The upperwing is brownish-black with white outer primaries, the under-wing white with moderately broad and sharply defined black margins. It may have a white cheek patch.

The flight of the grey-headed albatross is as other albatrosses. They are not keen on following ships.

Circumpolar, breeding on sub-Antarctic islands, the grey-headed albatross returns to the steep tussocky slopes, often in company with its close relative, the black-browed albatross, in October. Colonies are large, maybe as many as 10,000 pairs. The large nest is made of mud and grass, and holds a single egg, incubated for 72 days, the parents taking shifts of a week or two each. The white downy chicks are fed on squid, lampreys and other fish by regurgitation and they fledge at about 141 days. With a longer cycle than the black-browed, this species normally only breeds every other year. Sexually mature by their tenth year, they may live to 30.

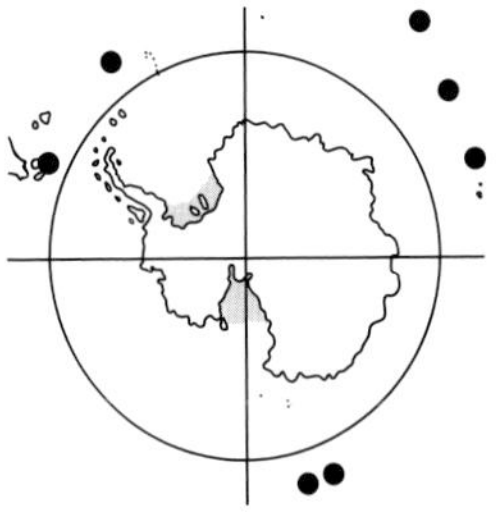

Dispersing widely, some birds work the Humboldt current to Peruvian waters in the winter. With a total world population in the region of 185,000, South Georgia is an important breeding station, but also Diego Ramirez, Campbell Island in the New Zealand sub-Antarctic, Kerguelen, Crozet and Prince Edward Islands on the edge of the Convergence. Egg-collecting may no longer be a threat, but commercial fishing activities have triggered a serious decline in the numbers of the species.

WINDS AND BLIZZARDS

Antarctic winds blow strongly, there is little in their way. At sea, the open and uninterrupted Southern Ocean offers a corridor for the prevailing 'west wind drift'. Closer to the continent and south of 55°, contrary currents create the 'east wind drift'.

In polar regions, the strongest are winds born in the cold air of the ice-cap, blowing down steep slopes and accelerating under gravity. These 'katabatic' (down-flowing) winds reach fearsome speeds, with 192km/h (120mph) common. In the 1911–14 Mawson expedition, the Australians recorded gusts of up to 224km/h (140mph), breaking their anemometer. These winds arrive with disconcerting suddenness, causing severe wind chill and difficult conditions for small boats, yet they cease as abruptly as they arrive. Gales following a snowstorm lift the new snow and create blizzards, when the driven snow has the erosive power of sand, penetrating everywhere, polishing rocks and making travel difficult or even impossible.

LIGHT-MANTLED SOOTY ALBATROSS

(Light-mantled, grey mantled albatross)
Phoebetria palpebrata

Length
78–89cm
(31–35in)
Wingspan
183–218cm
(72–86in)

An elegant and handsome sooty-brown with conspicuously grey-buff mantle and lower back, the light-mantled sooty albatross has a prominently dark head. Underparts are paler, but wings and tail are a matching sooty-brown. The black bill has a pale blue lateral groove on the lower mandible which is visible at close range. A semicircle of white feathers is behind the eye. (The more northern sooty albatross, which overlaps with this species in the southern Indian Ocean, lacks the grey-buff mantle and has a yellow-orange lateral groove on the lower mandible.)

In flight, light-mantled sooties are graceful, gliding

with occasional strong wingbeats. Slender by comparison with the giant petrels, they are less bulky and have 'pointed' wings and tail. They follow ships, sometimes for long periods, and patronise fishing vessels for offal.

They take their prey, mainly squid and krill, but other crustaceans, fish and carrion, too, by surface-seizing, as well as by diving and plunging below the surface, working especially at night.

Light-mantled sooties breed on islands from South Georgia to the New Zealand sub-Antarctic, returning to the steep slopes, cliff ledges or rocky cliffs, sometimes inland and amongst tussock or ferns, in September or October. Courtship includes the pair flying in close formation with highly synchronised aerobatics, calling with an eerie and wild two-note scream in sensuous abandon.

They nest in solitary fashion or in small loose-knit colonies. One egg is laid in October or November on a low cone of mud and vegetation, and incubation is for about 69 days by both parents working shifts of varying duration. The greyish chicks are fledged in about 141–170 days and go to sea in April or May. Breeding is biennial.

In winter light-mantled sooties are circumpolar and widely dispersed, common in waters south of the Convergence down to the pack-ice and north to Peru by way of the Humboldt current (also in large numbers in the Beagle Channel in winter). The total world population is possibly in the region of 20,000 breeding pairs. In the past they were much exploited for food.

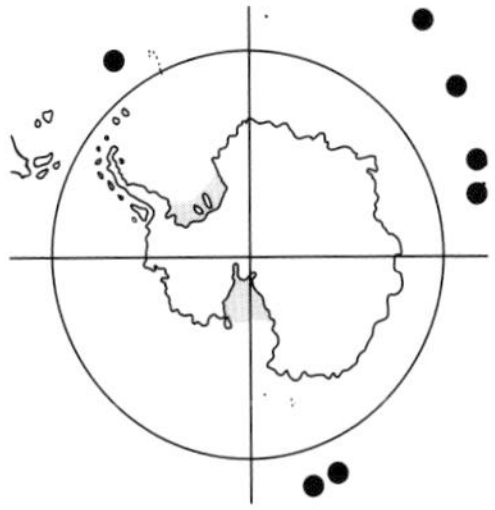

'... no music could be more apt to that romantic desolation. The very spirit of the place! A chord within responds, a chord held silent for a thousand decades while the ice-caps slowly died, and man set foot upon the path that may lead up from barbarism. Surprising that a sooty albatross calling to his mate in the cliffs can s end such ideas running through the mind.'
Leo Harrison Matthews, in South Georgia, 1926

'At 6 o'clock, having but little Wind, we brought to among some loose Ice, hoisted out the boats and took up as much as filled our empty Casks; while this was doing Mr Forster shott an Albatross whose plumage was of a Dark grey Colour, its head, upper sides of the Wings rather inclining to black with white Eye brows, we saw these Birds about the time of our first falling in with these Ice Islands and they have accompanied us ever since. Some of the Seamen call them Quaker Birds, from their grave Colour...'

Captain James Cook, on board HMS *Resolution*,
64°12S 38°14E, January 12 1773

PETRELS

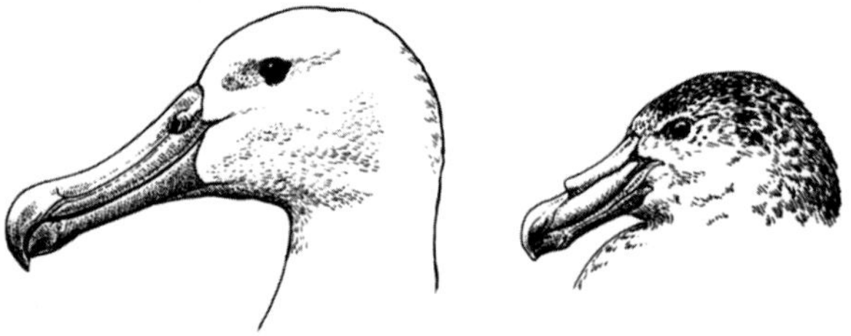

Tubenoses
The tubenose's 'tube' is concealed at the base of the bill, with openings either side in the albatrosses, while in the smaller petrels, from the southern giant petrel (illustrated right) downwards, it is placed high on the upper mandible.

From the mighty albatross to the diminutive storm-petrel, the petrels, or 'tubenoses', include many species in a wide-ranging group of families. They are characteristically marked by deeply grooved and hooked bills. Their long nostrils indicate a highly developed sense of smell, which is unusual among birds; indeed, they themselves exhibit a musky odour. In feeding, they store fish-oil in their stomachs, using it to regurgitate for their young or to spit at intruders in a highly effective defence. Superb and distinctive in flight, they are at a grave disadvantage ashore, where they waddle about in a clumsy manner. Only the giant petrels walk strongly on land, exploiting this unusual petrel facility to take terrestrial prey, especially carrion.

SALTY PROBLEMS
Seabirds have a particular problem when it comes to dealing with the quantity of salt which they inevitably ingest in both drinking and fishing. They absorb far more than is healthy for them and more than their renal system can deal with. The surplus is conveyed by a network of blood vessels into fine tubes connected with the nasal glands. This concentrated sodium chloride is in solution and drips constantly from the tip of the beak.

NORTHERN GIANT PETREL

(Hall's giant petrel)
Macronectes halli

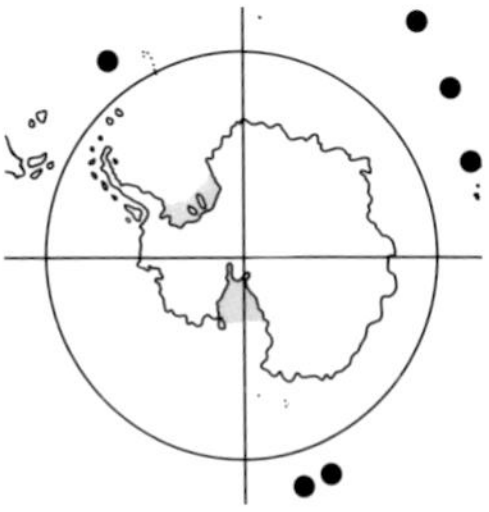

This species is only too easily confused with the southern giant petrel, with which it may hybridise, although a different breeding pattern and social behaviour confirm its status as a separate species. Underparts are more uniformly dark than on the southern species (the all-white morph is always the southern form), and the tip of the bill has a pinkish/reddish tinge which is diagnostic, although only visible at close range. Circumpolar, the northern giant petrel breeds on sub-Antarctic islands.

Length
81–94cm (32–37in)
Wingspan
102–112cm (71–79 in)

Giant petrel, from 'A General History of Birds', J A Latham, 1824

'...often seen sailing, with expanded wings, close to the surface of the water, without appearing to move them; like others of the Genus, said to be most active and in the greatest numbers, either in storms or at the approach of them; hence their appearance is unwelcome to the mariners.'

SOUTHERN GIANT PETREL

(Antarctic giant petrel, giant fulmar, stinker, nellie)
Macronectes giganteus

Length
86–99cm
(34–39in)
Wingspan
185–205cm
(73–81in)

The plumage of the southern giant petrel varies over a wide range from almost black to almost white, but is mainly grey. A small but significant proportion is more or less white all over. Juveniles are blackish-brown all over; as they age, their heads and breasts become progressively paler. The underparts are darker towards the tail. The bill colour, which is diagnostic, is dullish yellow with a green tip.

Enthusiastic ship-followers, southern giant petrels resemble small albatrosses in flight, but are less graceful: a few stiff-winged flaps are followed by short glides.

Giant petrels are scavengers, well described as the

'vultures of the Antarctic'. They gather sociably to feed on carrion of all sorts – whale carcasses, for instance – and they follow ships for galley waste, but they will also fish for krill and squid. They are closely associated with penguin and seal colonies which provide much of their food (as much as 50% of the food regurgitated to the chicks may be penguin carrion). In winter, fish and squid become more important food items.

The hooked bill of the giant petrel is a powerful tearing tool which is also an effective weapon, inflicting a painful wound. Another defensive mechanism, whether in chick or adult, is the ability forcibly to eject a noisome spit of oil which may reach a good metre from the bird, hence the name 'stinker'.

Breeding begins in October, the birds nesting sometimes alone and sometimes in loose colonies, tending to return to the same site. A large and conspicuous mound of stones, limpet shells and bits of vegetable matter is built on an exposed rock offering a high vantage point. One egg is laid in November, followed by an incubation period of around 60 days, with both sexes taking part in incubation and subsequent brooding. The downy chick is closely guarded for the first couple of weeks, after which it is left alone while the parents forage. It will fledge in early May.

Giant petrels are particularly vulnerable to disturbance at the nest and it is important to allow them plenty of space, quite apart from the advisability of avoiding the spewed oil which tends to foul clothes for a considerable time after the event! Although the species enjoys healthy populations it does not do well in areas colonised by scientific research stations. At sea, the birds suffer losses as an incidental by-catch of commercial fisheries.

Southern giant petrels are circumpolar, breeding both on the Antarctic Peninsula and the sub-Antarctic islands. While adolescent birds may wander the cold-water currents as far as the tropics, mature adults probably do not stray far from the breeding place. The current population is about 60,000.

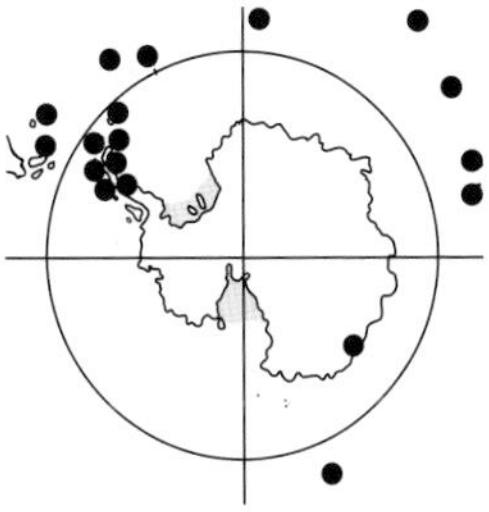

'Stinker'

'Stinker' from the offensive action of petrels when they eject a foul-smelling jet of stomach oil at anyone who approaches too close. Possibly also a name bestowed by the whalers from their unappetising behaviour at a carcass on the flensing plan, when they dig deep into the gaping flesh and reappear with bloodied head and neck and aggressively widespread wings.

'Nellie'

'Nosy nelly' is American slang for a person who pokes his nose where it is not wanted: in this case into bloody carrion.

SOUTHERN FULMAR

(Antarctic or silver fulmar, silver-grey petrel)
Fulmarus glacialoides

Length
46–50cm
(18–19½in)
Wingspan
114–120cm
(45–47in)

Superficially gull-like, fulmars are stockier in flight, bull-necked, sleek yet chunky. The stubby tubenose bill and dark eye shows at close range. The upperparts are mainly pale bluish-grey. The wings are conspicuously straight-edged and narrow, with a pale patch at the base of the primaries and a dark trailing edge. In flight they flap and glide, stiff-winged, wingbeats alternating with effortless banking, gliding and soaring. They are masters at gliding but flap readily enough in a calm.

Their natural food is small fish, squid and plankton, but fulmars have taken enthusiastically to following trawlers and whalers for offal. In 1847, Thomas Bewick wrote of their northern cousins as 'extremely greedy and gluttonous, they follow ships fearlessly for filth, they pursue the bloody track of wounded whale. Great flocks ravenously pluck off and devour lumps of blubber, till they can hold no more'.

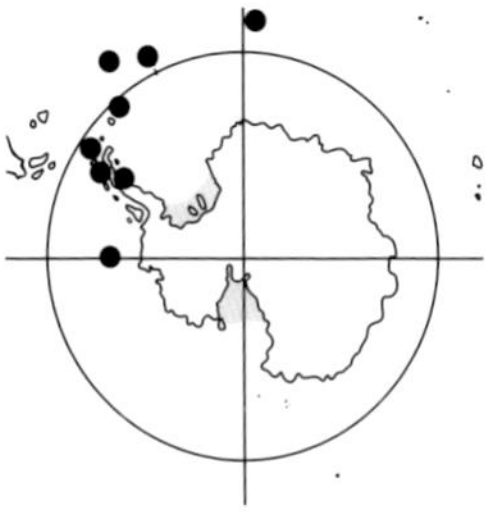

In courtship fulmars hold raucous water-dances near the breeding cliffs; they are equally noisy at the nest-scrape. They breed colonially, laying a single egg in November on a bare and often inaccessible ledge on exposed sea cliffs. Incubation is approximately 46 days; the chick is closely attended for three weeks and fledges at eight weeks. At the nest they will spit out a jet of stomach oil in the style of giant petrels as an offensive weapon. Mortality at the breeding grounds is mostly linked to weather conditions, such as freezing or flooding, but there is also some predation by skuas.

Adults range widely over the Southern Ocean. They are circumpolar and common year-round residents in the peninsula. Adolescents range to the sub-tropics by way of cold-water currents.

DISTANCES ACROSS THE SEA AND ICE

Visibility is often very good in Antarctica because there is virtually no dust in the air and little moisture in winds blowing in from the continent. As a result, judging distance is not easy and it may even be practical to multiply your estimates by as much as 5 or 6!

The unusual clarity of light gives rise to some interesting phenomena:

Parhelia are mock suns, symmetrically arranged coloured rings, sometimes known as sun-dogs.

Parselenae are mock moons.

Fogbows are related to rainbows, their colours varying with the size of waterdrops.

ANTARCTIC PETREL

Thalassoica antarctica

Length
40–46cm
(16–18in)
Wingspan
101–104cm
(40–41in)

Chocolate brown, mottled with white at the sides and rump, the Antarctic petrel is superficially like the cape petrel but larger and without the 'spattered white paint' effect on the upperwings. They are much less in evidence around ships, unless they are fishing vessels offering offal, but sometimes a few dozen will keep station for a while. Closer views of the upperwing pattern reveal the white trailing (sub-terminal) edge which distinguishes this species. In flight, usually well above the sea, it has the stiff gliding action alternating with wingbeats typical of fulmars.

Hovering over open water before a whole-hearted

plunge, often with outspread wings, Antarctic petrels seize krill, small fish and amphipods from the surface. In association with fishing or whaling vessels, they may gather in flocks of many thousands.

Antarctic petrels spend the austral winter at sea, more or less close to the pack-ice, returning in November to the colonial breeding grounds, mainly on inland mountains but also along the continental coast and most southerly islands. In November and until mid-December there is a marked passage of birds – sometimes in flocks of dozens – flying south along the Bransfield and Gerlache Straits.

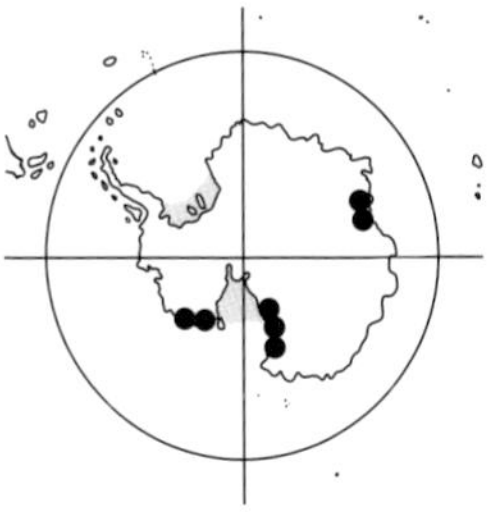

They nest in 'saucers' built on cliff ledges. One egg is incubated for 40–48 days, and the chick fledged in 42–47 days. Adolescent birds may reach up to South Africa or New Zealand but most adults remain not far from the ice.

The total population of the Antarctic petrel is several million pairs. Although they are mainly found in the region of the Ross Sea, there are also large colonies on mountain ranges around the base of the Weddell Sea.

CAPE PETREL

(Pintado or pied petrel, cape pigeon)
Daption capense

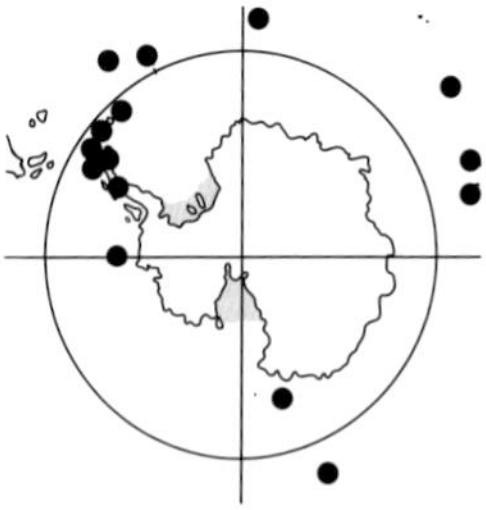

Circumpolar and abundant, cape petrels range widely over the Southern Ocean; in the austral winter they disperse north as far as the equator, returning to the colony in September/October. The bird has a potential lifespan of 15–20 years.

Length 38–40cm (15–16in)

Wingspan 81–91cm (32–36in)

Scattered white and brown chequerboard blotches on black wings, a sooty-black head and white underparts distinguish the cape petrel. Juveniles are as adults. It flies in fulmar fashion, a sequence of stiff flaps followed by gliding, in gregarious flocks, and is an enthusiastic ship-follower.

Squid, krill and fish are the main food, taken by day and night from the surface by pecking in a pigeon-like manner (hence the seaman's name cape pigeon) but sometimes by dipping in flight. Cape petrels commonly attend trawlers for offal, take galley waste from other ships and associate with whales for scraps.

In the breeding season the cape petrel frequents open inshore waters not too far from the colonies. Unlined nests are situated on exposed cliff ledges, crevices or among boulders. One egg, in November, is incubated for 41–50 days, and the chick fledged at 47–57 days. Severe weather is the main cause of each mortality, though skuas take some eggs and chicks.

SNOW PETREL

Pagodroma nivea

Snow-white plumage, coal-black eyes and short black bill make this bird unmistakable. Floating around pack-ice and icebergs, only its movement betrays its presence as a ghostly apparition: the snow petrel is highly manoeuvrable with a bat-like flight. Whiteness is a form of cryptic coloration, acting as a perfect camouflage in a world of ice and snow.

Snow petrels are more or less indifferent to ships. Their main food is krill, small fish and carrion taken on the wing in tern-style, but they will also forage for larger plankton animals from edges of older pack-ice.

Snow petrels are found only in association with the pack-ice and always south of 55° latitude. They are sedentary birds, never straying far from their home base. They breed in loose colonies, in crevices and hollows on mountain peaks and on nunataks. Returning to the nest sites in November, they may dig through a metre of snow to find the ground. One egg is incubated for 41–49 days; the chicks fledge in 41–54 days. Eggs and chicks may be taken by skuas, but extremes of weather are a more serious cause of mortality.

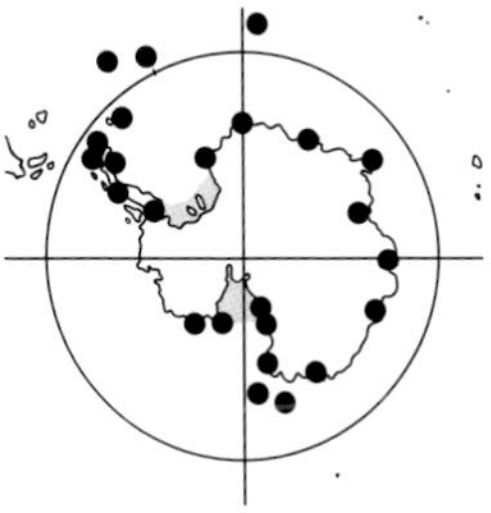

Circumpolar and abundant, the snow petrel is especially common in the Ross Sea. It has a lifespan of 14–20 years.

Length
30–35cm (12–14in)

Wingspan
76–79cm (30–31in)

WHITE-HEADED PETREL

(White-headed fulmar)
Pterodroma lessonii

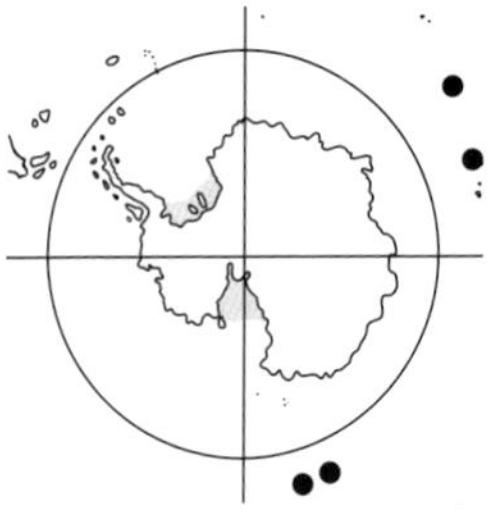

Length
40–46cm
(16–18in)
Wingspan
109cm
(43in)

This is the only petrel with a whitish head and tail; it has a dark eye-patch. With dark blue-grey plumage on the upperparts, an M-mark on the wing, a white rump, and white underparts except for a dark underwing, both adults and juveniles look alike.

The white-headed petrel is powerful and fast in flight, progressing in a series of wide-ranging arcs. It feeds mostly by night, taking squid, crustaceans and fish from the surface. It is not a ship-follower.

The adults return to the sub-Antarctic breeding islands in October, sometimes just one pair, sometimes in loose colonies. One egg is laid in an underground burrow in the tussock or scrub near the coast. Incubation takes approximately 60 days, with fledging in around 100 days, when the young birds disperse widely, though remaining south of latitude 30°S and down to the pack-ice.

The main stronghold of the species is at Kerguelen and Macquarie Islands, where it is heavily predated by feral cats, rats and skuas. It also competes with sooty shearwaters and rabbits for suitable burrows.

SOFT-PLUMAGED PETREL

(Soft-plumaged fulmar)
Pterodroma mollis

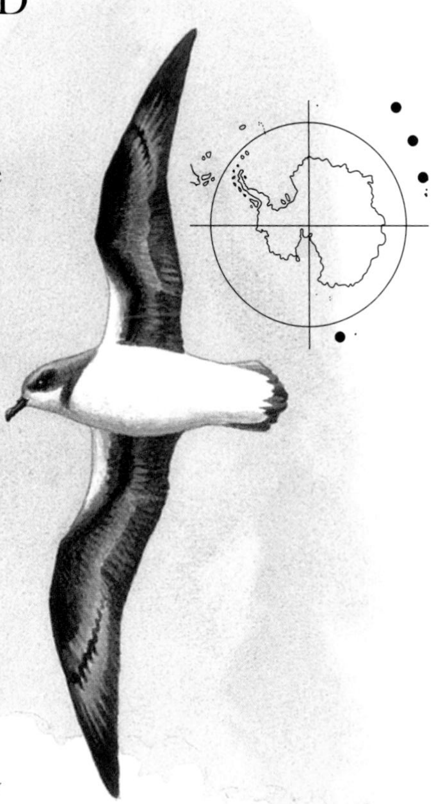

The soft-plumaged petrel may be recognised by its greyish-brown cap and forehead, with a white chin and throat, and a dark mask behind and above the eye; it has a grey breastband, grey upperparts and more or less white underparts. The upperwing is brown-grey, with dark primaries and crossed with an M-mark; the underwing is grey, with a pale central stripe. Juveniles and adults are alike. Lively in flight, the soft-plumaged petrel rushes about from side to side with fast wingbeats interspersed with gliding.

Not enthusiastic ship-followers, they may nevertheless be present in large flocks. They are sociable, feeding on the surface, taking mainly squid, krill and probably fish.

Adults return to oceanic islands from September, breeding colonially on steep tussocky coastal slopes. A single egg is laid in November or December in a burrow. Incubation takes about 50 days, with chicks fledging in around 90 days, dispersing in May over the South Atlantic and Indian Oceans.

Natural predators include skuas, but introduced cats and rats are a major problem for the species.

Length
32–37cm
(12½–14½in)

Wingspan
83–95cm
(32½–37½in)

BLUE PETREL

Halobaena caerulea

Length
28–30cm
(11–12in)
Wingspan
58–66cm
(23–26in)

The blue petrel has bluish-grey upperparts behind a white/grey forehead which merges into a dark crown; it has a dark grey collar. The upperwing is also bluish-grey with darker primaries forming an M-mark, while the underwing is paler and grey-edged. The square grey tail ends with a narrow black band tipped with white: this is the only petrel with a white tip to the tail. This, and the darker hooded head contrasting with the blue-grey body, separates it from the confusingly similar prions. It flies with stiff flaps and long glides.

A cold-water petrel of the sub-Antarctic and Antarctic, the blue petrel surface-feeds by dipping and seizing krill and other shrimps and small fish. Sometimes it attends ships, often in flocks, when it may be in association with huge numbers of prions from which it is not easy to distinguish.

Blue petrels return to the tussock slopes of sub-Antarctic islands in September, laying single eggs deep in underground burrows. The incubation period is 45–52 days. The chick is fledged by its 60th day; the young disperse in February or March as far north as Peru in the Pacific but less far north in the Atlantic and Indian Oceans. In adult years they are more sedentary.

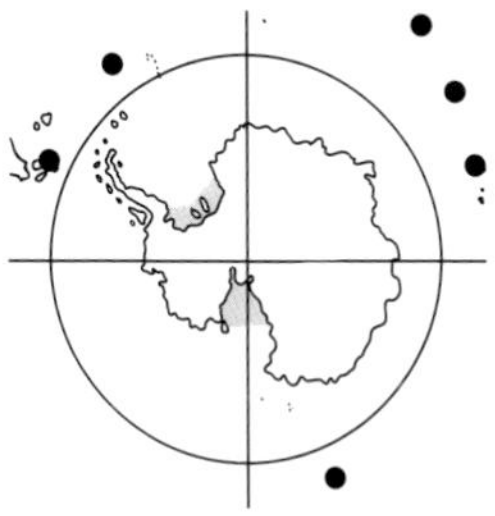

Skuas are the main predator on islands like Diego Ramirez (where they breed in huge numbers) Kerguelen, Prince Edward and Crozet. On other islands blue petrels have suffered greatly from introduced cats and rats. At sea giant petrels may take them.

OIL SECRETION AND EXCRETION

In addition to their large tail glands which yield oil for preening, all members of the petrel family, from the mighty albatross to the sparrow-sized storm petrel, regurgitate stomach oil through mouth and nostrils. The function of this discharge, which occurs when the bird is alarmed or stimulated in some way, such as by the appearance of a predator or its mate, and in preening and chick-feeding, is somewhat puzzling. In composition it resembles the preen gland oil, and the spermaceti oil of whales. It is rich in vitamins A and D and turns to wax when cold. It appears to be a dietary residue of the petrel's oil-rich fish and crustacean food, accumulated after the digestion of the more soluble protein component. The oil is stored in the stomach cells. It has an unpleasantly strong musky odour which clings persistently to the petrel and its nesting place (and to human flesh and clothes when an observer handles any petrel). In the fulmars, including the giant petrel of the southern oceans (appropriately named 'stinker'), the evil-smelling fluid may shoot several feet towards the visitor, as if deliberately aimed – although it is more likely that it travels in that direction because the bird is facing towards him, ready to defend itself with the hooked bill, which is opened threateningly. The main function of this vomiting is to lighten the bird for easier escape. The skunk-like habit of squirting a stinking fluid at intruders may have developed therefore as a supplementary defence in the fulmars, which nest in open vulnerable situations.

The oil appears only in the stomachs of nesting petrels, disappearing when the chicks are bigger and are being fed more solid semi-digested marine organisms; it is in effect a store of baby food of the right consistency. It has also been suggested that it serves the adult, thirsty during the typically long spells of incubation and brooding alone at the nest, as reserve 'physiologic water', camel-fashion. Despite its powerful smell, it is perfectly digestible, and is used in the preparation of food by Polynesian and other peoples.

BROAD-BILLED PRION

(Long-billed prion, icebird)
Pachyptila vittata

Prions, known to the early seamen as whalebirds because of the spectacular flocks which gathered to feed on the plankton disturbed by whale activity, are confined to the Southern Ocean. Small and blue-grey, they carry striking M-marks on their upper wings and have a black-tipped tail. Rather in the manner of the baleen whales they attend, they gulp water rich in copepods, and then force it out through a comb-like sieve (palatal lamellae) which acts as a filter along the side of the bill.

Length
25–30cm
(10–12in)
Wingspan
57–66cm
(22½–26in)

The characteristic blue-grey of prions is somewhat darker in this species, especially around the head. The white superciliary stripe sits on top of a longer black eye-stripe. The lower part of the head is white, giving a distinctive white chin effect. Upperparts are pale blue-grey and underparts white; the upperwing, too, is pale blue-grey, well marked with a broad and open M-mark. A blue-grey tail is tipped with black. From below, the tail has a dark streak extending inwards from the terminal black band. As its name suggests, this has the largest bill of the prions. Both juvenile and adult look similar. Flight is relatively slow.

The broad-billed prion flies low over the water with stiff wings, and feeds by pedalling with its feet across the water, dipping as it goes to scoop up small plankton prey. It often feeds in company with a huge flock, which may be mixed and may include storm-petrels. It is a moderately enthusiastic ship-follower.

It breeds colonially on coastal slopes and scree of islands all round the Southern Ocean and south of the South Shetlands, returning in July or August to lay a single egg in a burrow. Incubation takes around 50 days, fledging approximately a further 50 days. The young may winter as far north as Australia, South Africa and South America, while the adults are more sedentary, probably not going far from the breeding places, which they will visit occasionally, even outside the season.

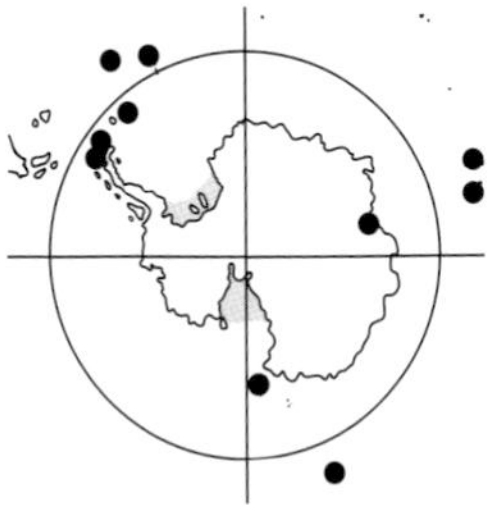

The main predators are skuas, except on islands where introduced cats and rats have caused havoc and seriously reduced their numbers.

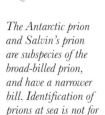

The Antarctic prion and Salvin's prion are subspecies of the broad-billed prion, and have a narrower bill. Identification of prions at sea is not for the faint-hearted!

The Antarctic prion *P. desolata* and Salvin's prion *P. salvini* are virtually similar seen at sea. Salvin's breeding base is the Crozet area and New Zealand sub-Antarctic Islands; that of the Antarctic prion includes the Falklands and South Georgia region. Birds of the prion genus *Pachyptila* are exceedingly difficult to tell apart at sea. For detailed descriptions see the excellent (but heavy!) Shirihai, Hadoram 2002 *A complete guide to Antarctic Wildlife*, Alula Press, which, in spite of its title, is a comprehensive guide to Antarctic and sub-Antarctic wildlife.

SLENDER-BILLED PRION

(Thin-billed prion)
Pachyptila belcheri

Length
25–26cm
(9¾–10¼in)

Wingspan
56cm
(22¼in)

The slender-billed prion is pale grey about the head; its most useful characteristic is the conspicuous white superciliary with a dark-grey stripe passing below and behind the eye. In flight, the open M-mark is less well defined than in the broad-billed, and the outer tail feathers are white. These prions are common, sometimes in large flocks, in Falkland and South Georgia waters. They are exceedingly difficult to determine at sea further south, though they frequently 'crash' on board ships in the dark.

FAIRY PRION

(Fulmar prion)
Pachyptila turtur

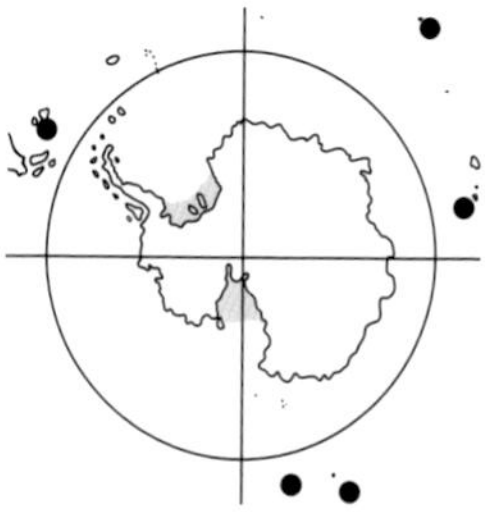

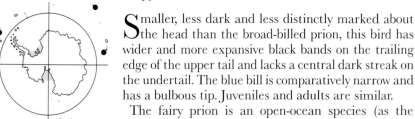

Smaller, less dark and less distinctly marked about the head than the broad-billed prion, this bird has wider and more expansive black bands on the trailing edge of the upper tail and lacks a central dark streak on the undertail. The blue bill is comparatively narrow and has a bulbous tip. Juveniles and adults are similar.

The fairy prion is an open-ocean species (as the broad-billed), except in foul weather, and is usually in close company and a large flock, often in association with other prions and storm-petrels. Buoyant in flight, it flutters with trailing legs to pick small items from the surface, mostly krill, copepods and amphipods. It is not a ship-follower except in the case of fishing vessels.

It breeds colonially on subtropical and sub-Antarctic islands. In September it returns to coastal cliffs, rock strewn and more open areas in which it can burrow. A single egg is laid from mid-October. Incubation takes approximately 55 days; fledging 43–56 days. Many fairy prions winter in the vicinity of the breeding grounds; others penetrate north as far as Australia and South Africa. Skuas are the natural predators.

Length
25–28cm
(10–11in)
Wingspan
56–60cm
(22–23½in)

The fulmar prion P. crassirostris is paler and has a more distinct wing-M. Its bill is shorter and stouter. Based on the New Zealand sub-Antarctic islands, it is virtually impossible to distinguish from the fairy prion at sea.

WHITE-CHINNED PETREL

(Shoemaker, cobbler, cape hen, spectacled petrel)
Procellaria aequinoctialis

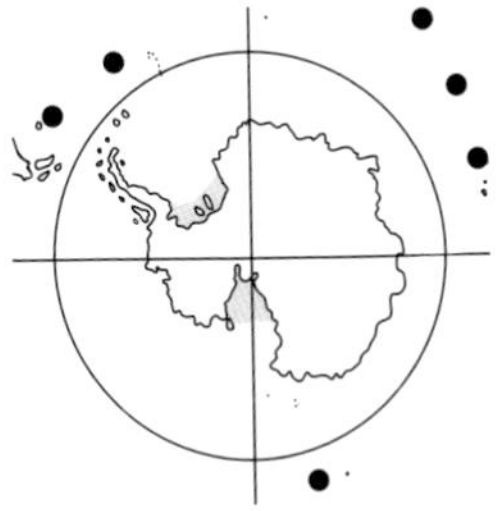

Length
51–58cm
(20–23in)
Wingspan
134–147cm
(53–58in)

The plumage of both adults and juveniles is black-brown all over, while there is a variable area of white around the face and chin, not always easily seen in flight. The bill is pale, with a black ridge (culmen) and stocky foreparts. This is a heavily built petrel with broad wings. In flight the legs project behind the wedge-shaped tail. Larger than the shearwaters, it has a strong flight, characterised by slow flapping and long glides, high over the waves.

The preferred food is squid and krill, but white-chinned petrels are confirmed ship-followers, taking galley waste but especially enthusiastic for trawler offal. Food is taken mainly from the surface by grabbing or by plunge-diving.

White-chinned petrels are one of the first birds to return to the sub-Antarctic breeding colonies, in October. (They do not nest on the Antarctic continent or the peninsular islands.) A single egg is laid in an underground burrow. The common name 'shoemaker' or 'cobbler' comes from their tendency to tap their bills in a hammering fashion at the burrow entrance when they come ashore at dusk. Incubation takes 57–62 days, and the chick is fledged in 87–106 days, when it disperses over the wide Southern Ocean, penetrating northwards only by way of the cold water Benguela and Humboldt currents and generally frequenting the disturbed waters of the Convergence and other upwellings.

White-chinned petrels are exceedingly common in sub-Antarctic waters; they are always in company with ships, along with sooty shearwaters, in the northern half of the Drake Passage and the Cape Horn region, for example. The total population is in the millions: over two million pairs breed on South Georgia. Islands with significant numbers of rats and cats are the least likely to enjoy breeding populations of these petrels.

Note: In Australasian waters this species is easily confused with the closely related and almost identical looking Parkinson's and Westland petrels, whose bills are rather more strikingly marked.

SNOW ALGAE

Red (sometimes green, rarely yellow) discoloration on the surface of the snow marks the presence of the snow algae *Chlamydomonas nivalis*, a primitive organism which finds home in the air spaces of the snow by virtue of nutrients carried to it by air. Wind-driven sea spray brings marine salts and atmospheric fallout provides sulphates and nitrates. In due course melting carries the algae to the sea where they enrich the mix and provide yet more sustenance for the plankton animals. (Beware confusing snow algae with penguin poop, which is very often stained krill-red!)

SOOTY SHEARWATER

(Muttonbird, titi)
Puffinus griseus

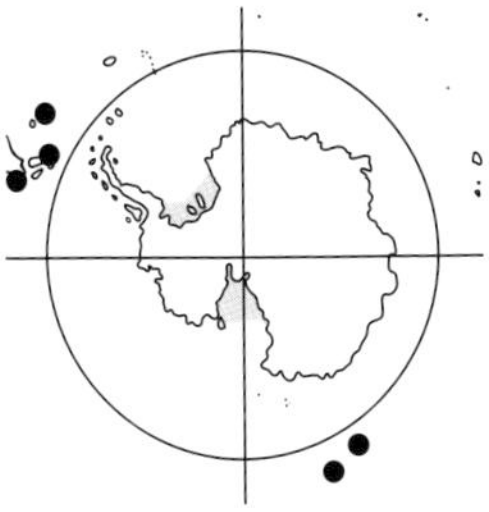

Apart from a greyish chin and throat and off-white flashes under the wing, sooty shearwaters are indeed sooty, though with an element of brown. Even the bill and legs are blackish-grey. The grooved and horny-plated bill is hooked for fish-catching. Juveniles and adults are similar. It has a strong flight, when the body appears stout and the wings are long and narrow; a few stiff flaps are followed by a long glide. Sociable birds, they are often in large flocks, both in flight and on the surface, where they gather in rafts, and they are frequently in company with other petrels and penguins. They are not ship-followers, except in the case of fishing vessels.

Length
40–46cm
(16–18in)
Wingspan
94–104cm
(37–41in)

The birds pursue squid and small fish in shallow plunge-dives from a low height or by seizing on the surface, but can fly underwater to an incredible 65m (205ft).

Sooty shearwaters range widely over the Pacific and the Atlantic. In the Southern Ocean they frequent the area of the Convergence and are usually in large numbers off Cape Horn. They were an abundant species, numbered in millions, breeding on islands off South America and Australasia, but are currently in decline.

They burrow to nest colonially on coastal slopes of the sub-Antarctic islands. The single egg is laid in November or December, and incubated for 53–56 days; the chick fledges in 86–106 days. While some adults may remain in the Southern Ocean for the austral winter, most birds migrate to high latitudes in both the Pacific and Atlantic. (The greatest concentration of sooties is in the North Pacific in the northern summer.) In the past they were much exploited for food.

'... insupportable stench from the deep bed of guano, which may at some period be valuable to the farmers of our Australasian colonies.'
James Clark Ross, in 1841, on finding 'inconceivable myriads of penguins'

GUANO

Seabird faeces are rich in organic nitrogen and phosphate: valuable dung, which encourages a lush growth of grasses and flowering plants. In wet climates these droppings are soon leached of their mineral richness, but on coasts they desiccate to become a potentially commercial crop.

Guano is an Inca word for the naturally desiccated dung of fish-eating sea fowl – cormorants, boobies, pelicans and penguins. Prehistoric Peruvian farmers used the nitrogen-rich guano to improve their crops. The Incas protected the birds and extracted the guano on a sensible basis, taking it at a rate slower than it was produced. Later harvesters killed the golden goose with the usual enthusiasm.

From the early 19th century guano was a major product of international trade. Between 1848 and 1875 more than 20 million tons were shipped to Europe and the United States. In the early 20th century the deposits began to fail, with dire effects on the Peruvian economy. From 1909 a more sensible policy was pursued and the guano treated as a crop instead of a limitless resource. The seabird islands became sanctuaries, with walled defences against pests, stabilising the situation.

WILSON'S STORM-PETREL

(Yellow-webbed storm-petrel, Jesus-bird)
Oceanites oceanicus

Sooty-brown, but with a conspicuous white rump and a square tail, Wilson's storm-petrel has wings the same sooty-brown but with a narrow band of grey across the greater coverts (inside the primaries). A 'sea-going house martin', it flies like a butterfly with shallow, fast wingbeats. Sometimes the legs project behind the tail, but the yellow webs on the feet are

Length
15–19cm
(6–7½in)
Wingspan
38–42cm
(15–16½in)

best seen when the bird is in the hand (and they not infrequently come to grief on ships' decks at night).

In feeding, the bird skips, walks and patters over the surface, sometimes stopping for a moment with wings raised high and legs dangling, sometimes actually going backwards. Storm-petrels may be so called because they are often in close attendance on ships in foul weather. The word 'petrel' is from the Christian name Peter, deriving from the storm-petrels' habit of 'walking on water' in biblical style, a behaviour which also led to the popular name Jesus-bird. Early mariners called them 'Mother Carey's Chickens' and said that they were standing by to carry off the souls of drowned sailors in a reincarnation; the name may thus be associated with Mater Cara, the blessed virgin. In Peru they are known as *bailarines* – ballet dancers.

This petrel is not named for Edward Wilson, the artist/doctor of Scott's expeditions, but for Alexander Wilson, an equally distinguished Scottish/American ornithologist author of the early 19th-century 'American Ornithology'.

Solitary yet gregarious, Wilson's storm-petrels are often alone, often in flocks of hundreds. Feeding flocks may be in huge numbers, usually over the shallow water of the continental shelf, and millions forage around the pack-ice. They are opportunistic feeders, and enthusiastic ship and whale-followers, but krill is an important item of diet and Wilson's storm-petrel is indefatigable in search of krill concentrations. Downwind of whale-blows it scoops grease or oily matter from the condensed breath, and in company with a decomposing whale it will submerge to take an oil droplet as it rises to the surface. It is probably capable of smelling its way to carrion and its food potential. Flocks will crowd enthusiastically around galley waste, sucking oily drops.

Circumpolar, widespread and abundant, with a total population well into the millions, this is the most commonly recorded storm-petrel in Antarctic waters and possibly the most numerous seabird in the world with a population of maybe six million (though most people will never see one!).

Storm-petrels venture ashore only to breed and they take care to arrive and depart during the hours of darkness, if possible, because of the unwelcome attentions of predators like gulls and skuas. They arrive at the breeding grounds in November or December, nesting on rocky islets, cliffs and boulder scree and on ice-free areas above beaches. A single egg is laid in late December or early January in a burrow or small crevice, or under boulders, sometimes on bare ground but most often in a place offering protection from marauding gulls and skuas. The burrow may be just above the tideline or up on inland ridges and clifftops. Storm-petrels will even take readily to artificial nest sites such as stone piles, fish boxes, barrels, etc. The scrape may be lined with a few pebbles, bits of moss, lichens and penguin feathers. Both parents incubate for 39–48 days, and the chick hatches late January to late February. Should the burrow entrance be blocked by a snowfall, parents may dig through as much as 20cm (8in) to reach the entombed chick and feed it with stomach-oil. The prolonged breeding season may ensure that at least some young birds survive in seasons when snowfalls cause heavy mortality. Fledging at 54–69 days, mainly in early April, it is then abandoned by its parents. Starving, it finishes moulting into its flying suit and emerges at night to fly off to sea alone. In a month or so it migrates north to the other side of the planet.

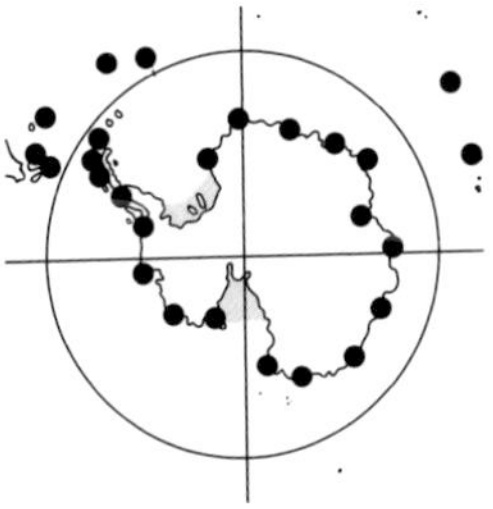

Wilson's storm-petrels winter as far north as the Californian and New England coasts, the Newfoundland Banks, Brittany, the Gulf of Aden, the Red Sea and the northwest Indian Ocean – areas of high plankton counts. One of the world's long-distance migrants, it is not much bigger than a sparrow. They are sometimes blown inland by a gale of wind, when the phenomenon of bedraggled and clumsy birds staggering about in the lights of city streets is known as a 'wreck'.

On some sub-Antarctic islands the introduced cats and rats take a severe toll. Skuas take some in flight. Whaling activity probably benefited the storm-petrels in the past, and the subsequent abundance of krill has furthered their success. However, krill exploitation by man may cause future problems.

BLACK-BELLIED STORM-PETREL

Fregetta tropica

Length
20cm (8in)
Wingspan
46cm (18in)

The black-bellied storm-petrel has strongly contrasting plumage, mainly black, with black bill, legs and feet, but the chin and rump and upper-tail coverts are white, and the black breast extends a thick black line down through a white belly to unite with the black tail. There are triangular white coverts on the underwing. Both sexes, including juveniles, are alike.

Significantly larger than the much commoner Wilson's, it flies close to the sea, dashing to left and right and frequently splashing its belly in the water only to leap clear with legs dangling. It patters over the water, dipping and plunging for small stuff – fish and cephalopods.

A determinedly pelagic bird, much less enamoured of inshore waters than Wilson's, the black-bellied storm-petrel comes ashore only at breeding time, patronizing offshore islands and stacks where it is least subject to predation. It is a rare visitor to the South Shetlands. Loose colonies nest in crevices and burrows amongst rocks, where a single egg is incubated for 38–44 days; the chick fledges in 65–71 days. Dispersal takes them north into all three oceans as far as the tropics and even the equator.

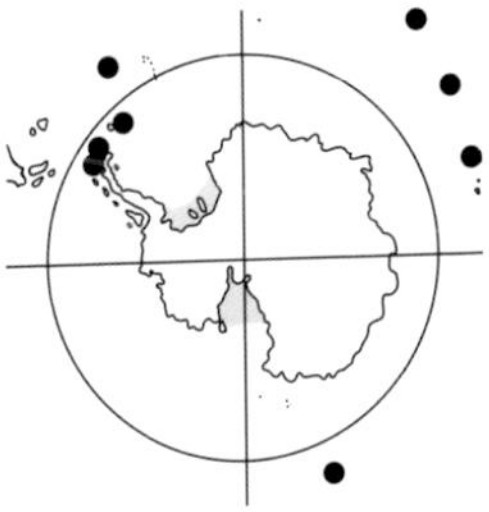

GREY-BACKED STORM-PETREL

Oceanites nereis

Length
16–19cm (7in)
Wingspan
39cm (15in)

The grey-backed storm-petrel is strongly marked, with ash-grey upperparts, white underparts, grey rump and upper tail with a black bar. It follows fishing boats and, less frequently, other vessels, taking planktonic crustaceans, small squid and fish while in flight or pattering over the surface.

The bird is circumpolar, sub-Antarctic, to be found from the Falklands east to the Chatham Islands, but mainly on the islands around New Zealand. It returns to breed in loose colonies during October and November, nesting in a tunnel of vegetation or a rocky crevice. A single egg is laid in November or December, with the chick fledging in April or May.

DIVING-PETRELS

Diving-petrels are stocky birds, black above and white below, short necked and small winged, with short legs housed well aft. They have broad-based and hook-tipped bills.

Where most petrels flap and glide, diving-petrels buzz about the sky in perpetual motion. They fly underwater and in the air with equal facility, as 'flying penguins'. All in all, they look remarkably like the little auks of similar, but northern, latitudes, a classic example of convergent evolution in which animals which are not related grow to look and act like each other as a response to similar environments. One striking difference in behaviour, though, is the way in which diving-petrels treat a wave when flying low over the sea. The rapid whirring flap of their short strong wings is laboured in the air but is most efficient underwater. Meeting a wave, they simply fly straight through it and out the other side.

The two Antarctic diving-petrels are difficult to tell apart at sea. In the hand, seen from above, the common diving-petrel's bill (top) is significantly narrower than that of the south Georgian diving-petrel (below). Their paired tube nostrils open upwards instead of forwards and are protected from the water in an adaptation for diving.

To overcome their natural buoyancy, diving-petrel bones are more solid than those of land birds; thus they float low in the water with little freeboard. When actively fishing they fly low, then dive headlong, expelling air from their lungs and compressing their plumage by muscular contraction. Their heart beats more slowly and oxygen is liberated from the blood and musculature. An average dive lasts less than a minute. Their prey is small fish and crustaceans, which they accumulate in a throat-pouch to take back to the nest.

Diving-petrels are rarely far from their breeding station in cold southern waters. They roost freely at sea, singly or in rafts, and are not ship-followers, though they often collide with a vessel at night in inshore waters, confused by the lights and ending up on deck. (Keep them in a box till morning, before releasing.) Much as the storm-petrels, they breed early, in their second year, in underground burrows in dense colonies, but unlike other petrels, chicks are brooded for the first ten days, then visited daily. They are nocturnal at the breeding grounds in the hope of avoiding skuas and gulls. In the past they were taken in large numbers for food.

SOUTH GEORGIAN DIVING-PETREL

Pelecanoides georgicus

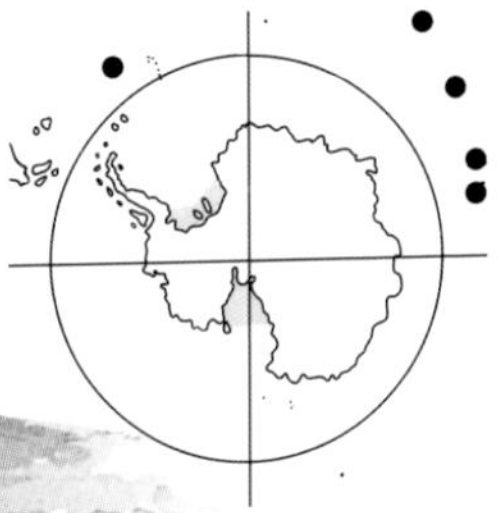

Length
18–21cm
(7–8in)

Wingspan
30–33cm
(12–13in)

Slightly smaller than the common diving-petrel, the Georgian diving-petrel is almost identical in appearance and they are virtually inseparable when seen at sea. It is only when you have them in the hand (and they not uncommonly come aboard ships at night, to be found skulking in a corner in the morning) that they are easily told apart by their bill shapes (see drawing opposite).

These diving-petrels are confined to the sub-Antarctic, breeding on oceanic islands from South Georgia by way of the Indian Ocean to southern New Zealand, and returning to their colonies in October. A single egg is laid in a chamber at the end of a burrow in scree or volcanic ash, or in sand dunes. Incubation takes 44–52 days; fledging 43–60 days.

Georgian diving-petrels are probably somewhat sedentary and abundant in their range (some two million pairs breed on South Georgia). On some islands they have suffered severely from the depredations of introduced cats; on Auckland Island they are extinct because Hooker's sea lions bulldozed their burrows.

COMMON DIVING-PETREL

Pelecanoides urinatrix

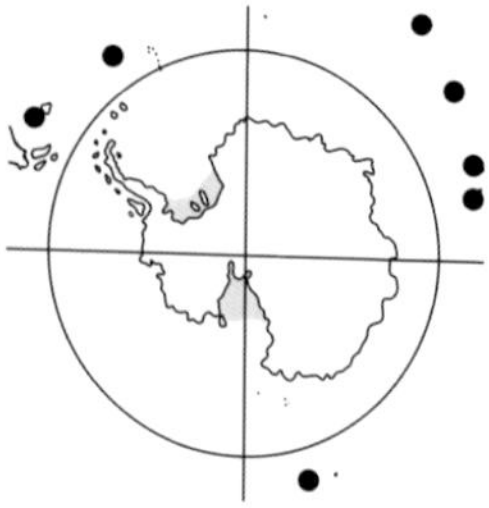

The common diving-petrel bears a remarkably close resemblance to the northern little auk: black about the head, except for some mottled grey about the ears, neck and throat; the chin and throat may be white. Upperparts are black, underparts mostly white. The upperwing is brown rather than black, the underwing black and grey. The tail is black above, greyer below.

Both pelagic and found in inshore waters, the common diving-petrel breeds in coastal colonies on oceanic islands from the Falklands by way of the Indian Ocean to southern New Zealand.

Length
20–25cm
(8–10in)
Wingspan
33–38cm
(13–15in)

The breeding season varies according to the location, between August and December. Colonies are established on the coasts of oceanic islands, where a single egg is laid in a burrow on steep tussocky slopes, or sometimes on flat ground. Incubation takes 53–55 days; fledging 45–59 days.

ANTARCTIC SHAG

(Imperial cormorant, king cormorant,
imperial shag, blue-eyed shag, Antarctic cormorant)
Phalacrocorax atriceps bransfieldensis

Length
72cm (28in)
Wingspan
124cm (49in)

Shags and cormorants are members of a large family of some 30 species which has successfully colonised the coastal regions of the world. There is a certain amount of confusion involved in the names, but the fact is that the terms are interchangeable, both shags and cormorants belonging to the same family – the Phalacrocoracidae.

The Antarctic shag, better known to most sailors in West Antarctica as the blue-eyed shag, is more or less blue-black all over, with a certain amount of white under the eyeline and down to the throat. In the breeding season the adult bird has a white dorsal patch, bright orange nasal caruncles – fleshy appendages ahead of the eyes – and a striking orbital ring which is cobalt blue. The colour fades at the end of the season, though it is still distinctive. Juveniles are duller and browner.

It forages sociably, flying in flocks, often swimming and diving synchronously. It feeds mainly on fish, but also crustaceans, squid and bottom-living invertebrates, caught by underwater chase after a jack-knife dive.

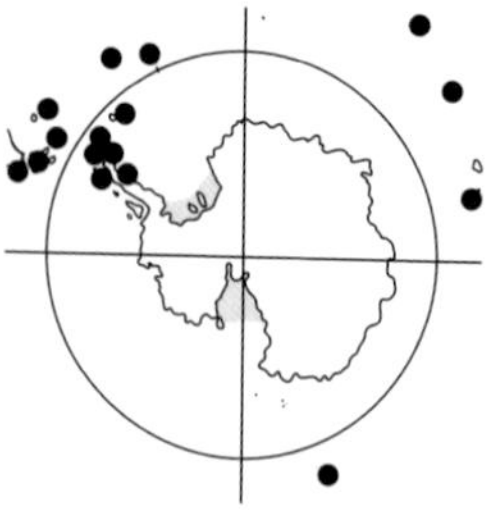

In several slightly different subspecies the blue-eyed shag ranges from the coasts of southern South America to the Antarctic mainland by way of the sub-Antarctic islands and the Antarctic Peninsula. They are sedentary birds, though they disperse to nearby waters in the winter. Continental and peninsular populations move north to open water. In South Georgia, the subspecies georgianus has marginally less white on the head and back.

On the whole it remains close inshore to the coast and islands, breeding colonially, sometimes just a few, sometimes several hundreds, on low sea-cliffs, rocky slopes or scree, or even on flat ground. Occasionally it is to be found alongside or even amongst nesting penguins.

The nest is a bulky cone of seaweed, feathers and almost anything else, including mummified chick corpses, bits of driftwood, etc, cemented with excrement. Both sexes build, though the female does the more intricate weaving. They tend to return to the same nest site, although not so often to the same mate, each year. Usually two or three eggs are laid from October even to mid-January. Both sexes incubate (28–31 days) though the males do most of the work. The chick is born naked, and brooded by either parent till it is over three weeks old when it is watched for yet another three weeks. Sheathbills patrol and scavenge in search of dropped food items when chicks are being fed. Skuas sometimes indulge in an aerial chase, forcing returning parents to disgorge their catch. The chicks fledge in about seven weeks, when the young birds tend to gather in sociable flocks on ice floes or convenient slopes close to the waterline. Breeding success is closely related to the relative abundance of available food, though skuas take some eggs and chicks. Some fledglings may be taken by leopard seals.

Even during the Antarctic summer, when most of the 24 hours enjoy daylight, shags return to roost in the traditional manner, before sunset. In this cold climate, they do not spread their wings to dry after diving in the manner so well known in temperate and tropical regions. Their inner plumage is extra dense.

SNOWY SHEATHBILL

(American sheathbill, greater sheathbill, paddy)
Chionis alba

Length
40cm (16in)
Wingspan
79cm (31in)

A dumpy, pigeon-like shorebird, the snowy sheathbill's plumage is entirely white. It has short, stout blue-grey or pink legs, the toes having only vestigial webs, a surprising feature for a bird found in the Antarctic. The blunt bill is covered with a horny yellow-green sheath which hides the nostril openings. There are pink-white wattles about the face. The wings are small, with sharp carpal spurs used in territorial fighting.

Snowy sheathbills are something of a surprise and an enigma, since it is not clear where they fit into the comfortably ordered system devised by Linnaeus. Even now taxonomists are unsure of their classification. The most widely held view is that they link the shorebirds (waders) and the gulls and skuas. Of the two species in the family only this one is common in the maritime Antarctic and sub-Antarctic. (The lesser

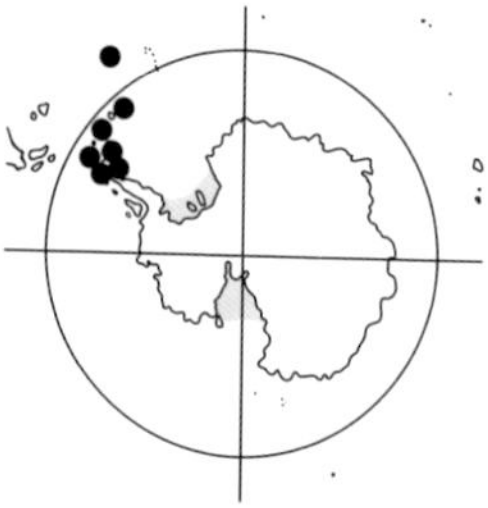

sheathbill is confined to the sub-Antarctic islands of the Indian Ocean and is a far more sedentary bird.)

Snowy sheathbills inhabit the Antarctic Peninsula and the islands of the Scotia Arc, through the South Orkneys and South Georgia. Looking like white pigeons, they strut about pecking for titbits in the manner of a farmyard fowl. They are scavengers and kleptoparasites, getting much of their food by stealing what has already been taken by penguins and shags.

Foraging amongst concentrations of penguins and shags, they take eggs and small chicks; often they stand by at feeding sessions, when they grab bits of food which are dropped during the regurgitation process. Penguins feed their young with part-digested krill 'balls' and the sheathbills excel in intercepting them. They take readily, too, to food offered at expedition bases and campsites. They also feed on bird and seal faeces, carrion, small limpets and the extruded stomach linings of penguins.

They breed as far south as 65°, returning to the territory in October/November. They nest in dark caves or crevices where there is an overhang – scree burrows, under huts or in empty huts, spaces between abandoned fuel drums and the detritus of scientific stations. The nest is a bulky, compacted mass of moulted penguin and gull feathers, dead chicks, bones, pebbles, limpet shells, moss, lichens and weed. Mainly solitary at nesting time, snowy sheathbills tend to be in close association with gentoos or chinstrap penguin or shag colonies, close to the sea, often on a ridge overlooking the colonies which provide their food. Two to four eggs, laid in December/January, are incubated by both parents for 29 days and fledged in 7–9 weeks, in late February. Most pairs only succeed in raising one or two chicks.

Although they are expert at avoiding the vicious pecks of penguins, one of the main causes of sheathbill mortality is that an accumulation of mud or ice on their feet or primary feathers may hamper their operations to such an extent that they succumb.

While sheathbills are markedly reluctant to fly, they are nevertheless strong in flight. In the austral winter they make long migratory flights, crossing the Drake Passage to congregate in groups numbering hundreds around Tierra del Fuego, Patagonia and the Falklands. Not averse to assisted passage on ships, they have enjoyed galley scraps sailing from ports in the Falklands and Argentina – and in one case crossing the Atlantic to a landfall at Plymouth in the British Isles.

SKUAS

The name 'skua' comes from the Icelandic *skufr* and is presumably a rendering of their chase-calls in flight. Skuas look superficially like immature gulls, but they are heavier, more robust and menacing in mien, as befits birds of prey. They have conspicuous white patches at the base of the primaries. Theirs is a piratical nature and they have hawk-like beaks to serve it.

Half a dozen species in two genera breed in the high latitudes of both hemispheres. Much learned discussion revolves around the question of how many species are present in the deep south, since distinct populations exist on various island groups. In Antarctica, the main contenders are the south polar skua and the brown skua, the southern version of the great skua. While they are generally accepted as distinct species it is often not in the least easy to separate them in the field, when their distribution overlaps, as in the peninsula, and where they occasionally hybridise as *Catharacta maccormicki x lonnbergi*.

Brown skua, Ross Island. Field sketch by Edward Wilson, 'Discovery' expedition, April 1902.

Skuas like to bathe in freshwater pools.

> 'They shake and splash and ruffle out their feathers quite in the manner of songbirds at a fountain.'
>
> Robert Cushman Murphy

SOUTH POLAR SKUA

(McCormick's skua)
Catharacta maccormicki

South polar skuas at Cape Adare

Length
53cm (21in)
Wingspan
127cm (50in)

The most southerly birds in the world, south polar skuas appear in three morphs (genetically based colour variants or phases): dark, intermediate and light, the paler version becoming commoner in the deep south. The dark morph has a dark brown-blackish head with a pale area at the base of the bill; the upperparts are a uniform blackish-brown, the underparts slightly paler. The light morph has a much paler head, pinkish-brown to greyish-white, with a pale collar at the back of the nape. The sides of the neck may have golden streaks. The upperparts are a uniform brownish-black, the underparts pale pink-brown to grey-white. Wings are brownish-black with the characteristic skua white patches at the base of the primaries. The tail is blackish; bill, legs and feet are blackish-grey.

This skua is named after Robert McCormick, the surgeon-naturalist who sailed with James Clark Ross in 'Erebus'.

Any skua with a pale nape and underparts contrasting with darker, uniform upperparts will be a south polar skua. They often follow ships and will freely and fearlessly perch on rails or deck.

As birds of prey and kleptoparasites, they are opportunistic feeders, but sea-fish and krill are a major part of their prey. Surface feeders, they swim and grab, but sometimes dip or plunge-dive in the fashion of terns. The main fish prey is the Antarctic herring *Pleurogramma antarcticum*, which itself feeds on copepods and ice-krill. They are enthusiastic predators on penguin, shag and tern colonies, and will chase shags, forcing them to disgorge in flight, but they are less dependent on piracy and less proficient at taking penguin chicks than the brown skua. They may take Wilson's storm-petrels in flight.

South polar skuas become sexually mature at five years old. Much attached to traditional nesting sites, they return to the breeding places, often close by bird cliffs or penguin rookeries, in late October and November. The nest is anything from an unlined scrape to a saucer of grasses, lichens and moss. It is often situated in solitary splendour on a high vantage point overlooking a substantial territory in the style of an eagle. Yet again, it is sometimes in loose colonies associated with nearby penguin rookeries. South polar skuas return to the same nest site year after year and are faithful to a long-term mate, normally pairing for life. The clutch size is largely dependent on the availability of food. In a good season, when there is plenty of krill, there will be two full-sized eggs; otherwise the second egg is likely to be smaller (or not laid at all) and laid a couple of days later. Eggs may be laid any time between late November to mid-February, again depending on food potential. Both sexes share the incubation period of approximately 30 days. The chicks are brooded by the males and attended assiduously, the parents being very aggressive in defence of the nest and young, not hesitating to attack a man, beating him about the face with wings or feet, or ripping his scalp in a power-dive (behaviour taken advantage of by researchers who trap them by lifting a hand net as the bird approaches). Fledging takes 57 days and is achieved some time between late February and early April; the success rate depends heavily on food availability.

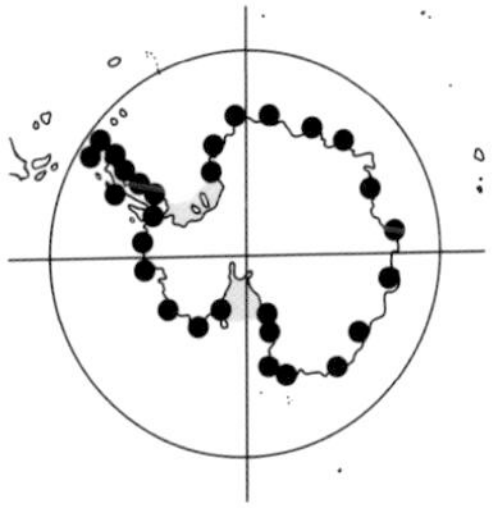

South polar skuas are circumpolar and abundant, mainly around the continent and the peninsula. They range far over the polar ice. While adolescent birds may disperse as far as the North Pacific and Atlantic Oceans, the adults remain closer to the breeding grounds through the austral winter.

BROWN SKUA

(Antarctic skua)
Catharacta antarctica

Length 61–66cm (24–26in)

Wingspan approximately 150cm (60in)

At first sight, the brown skua has the look of a heavyweight juvenile gull. Large and powerful, with a heavy body and a fierce manner, it has a brown head, almost always with dark cap and yellow streaks on the nape, lacking the 'collar' effect of the south polar skua. The upperparts are dark brown and flecked buff/pale yellow/rufous. Underparts are similar but greyer. The upperwing is blackish-brown with a marked white patch at the base of the primaries; the underwing is dark brown with an even more marked white patch. The tail is dark brown, the bill, legs and feet blackish-grey.

The brown skua displays piratical behaviour, pursuing shags and terns in flight, grabbing wings or tails and forcing them to disgorge their catch. It also takes carrion and follows ships for galley waste and fish offal. Often enough it will perch freely and fearlessly on deck. Ashore, they defend a feeding territory – a penguin colony for instance – vigorously. Sometimes they will forage, in co-operation with another skua, for penguin eggs, chicks and carrion.

Eggs may be carried off, small chicks swallowed whole on the spot, large ones dragged away. Given the opportunity, they will take shrimps from a melt pond, but mostly their krill comes second-hand by way of spillage, when adult penguins are feeding their young.

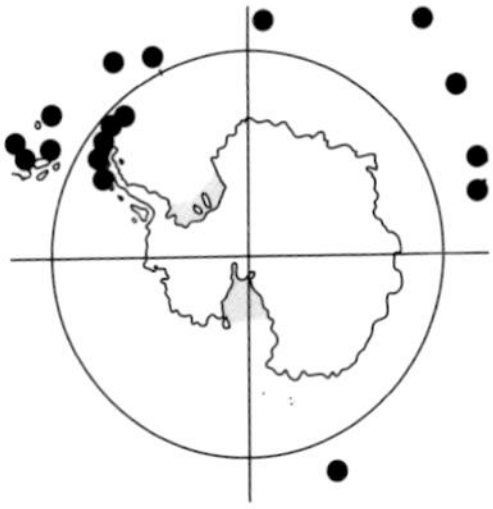

Brown skuas return to the breeding territory in late October and November, establishing the nest within convenient distance of penguin (or sometimes shag) colonies, and usually well away from other skuas. The nest is a simple scrape, often marked by a luxuriant algal or plant growth, and surrounded by the remains of food, eggshells, chickfeet and bones. They are faithful to the nest sites and to their mates, diligent in defence of both nesting and feeding areas.

Normally two eggs are laid from late November to early January. Incubation takes 30 days. The chicks are brooded by both parents and fledge from late March even into April. Dispersal is to the coasts of South America, South Africa and Australia in the austral winter.

Brown skuas are circumpolar, breeding mainly on the sub-Antarctic islands but also along the peninsula to 65°S.

Field sketch by Edward Wilson, 'Discovery' expedition, April 1902

KELP GULL

(Dominican gull, southern black-backed gull)
Larus dominicanus

Length
58cm (23in)
Wingspan
128–142cm
(50–56in)

The only gull in the Antarctic, the kelp gull is the southern version of the ubiquitous black-backed gulls of the north (but it is abundant and widely scattered through the southern hemisphere, almost to the Equator). In the fully adult bird of five years, the head is white, the saddle black and the rump white; underparts are white, and the upperwing black with a white trailing edge and the characteristic white 'mirror' at the outer edge. Juveniles moult through the usual stages of brown/grey.

Abundant, widely distributed and conspicuous, kelp gulls forage the coast and inshore waters. They have a close relationship with limpets. At the extreme south of their range, limpets *Nacella concinna* are their main food: Antarctic beaches and shore slopes are littered with the ravaged shells. The live limpet is superbly adapted to life in a cold climate, enjoying grazing on algae above the waterline in ice-free summers and migrating below the ice in wintertime. It is protected from freezing by a coat of antifreeze mucus. But kelp gulls patrol the tide's edge at low water, swimming and searching for active limpets, taking them by reaching or plunging. The molluscs are swallowed whole, the shells later regurgitated intact, littering the nest area in neat piles. Around scientific stations kelp gulls hope for scrap food, remembering the days before new regulations forbade feeding wildlife. They also fish for krill.

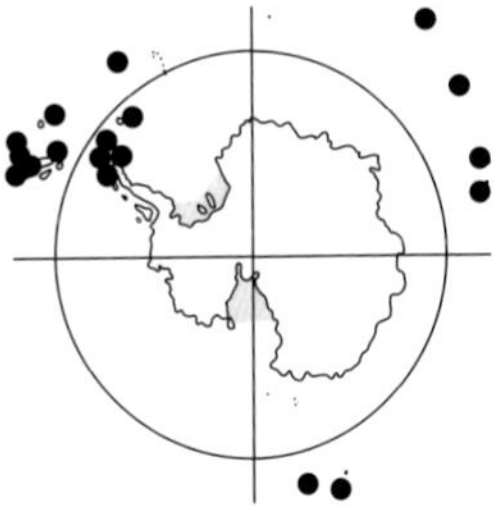

Kelp gulls nest colonially along rocky heights and cliffs close to the sea, and are not seriously attached to traditional sites. The nest structure is of vegetation, sometimes just a scrape, a bowl of mosses, lichens and grass, odds and ends of shells, seaweed, etc. The normal clutch is of two or three eggs, laid from late November. Incubated by both parents for 28 days, the eggs hatch in mid-December to late January. They are brooded by both parents, fledging from mid-January.

The chicks are not fed on limpets, but on small fish, mainly the young Antarctic herrings *Pleurogramma antarcticum* which are found near the surface and are suitably small. The chicks associate closely with their parents for many weeks after fledging. In the early stages of breeding, they suffer predation by south polar skuas and are particularly vulnerable to human disturbance, when they are inclined to desert the nest, allowing skuas or other gulls to take eggs or chicks.

Adult birds are likely to be resident in the Antarctic through the winter, sustained by limpets. Adolescent juveniles migrate north to South America in their first winter.

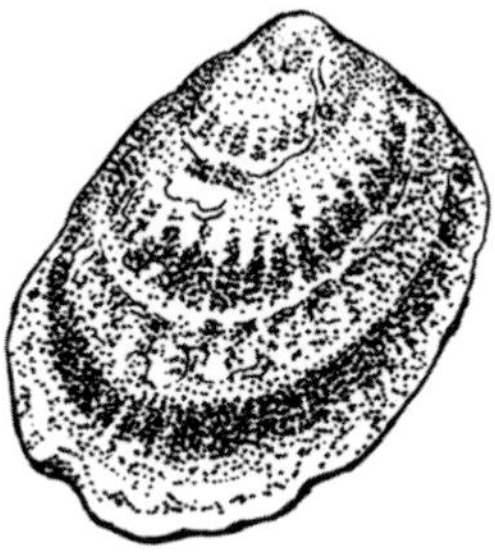

Kelp gull nests are surrounded by large numbers of limpet shells.

TERNS

There are over forty species of tern, from the Arctic to the Antarctic. Most are birds of the coast, some are oceanic. They are smaller, more graceful and more streamlined than the gulls which they superficially resemble, but they have narrower, more pointed wings and slender, sharp-pointed bills. Many have deeply forked tails, earning them the sailor's name of sea-swallow. They are short in the legs with small webbed feet; buoyant on the sea yet rarely in it, for they swim poorly. They often enjoy a rest on a piece of driftwood or raft of seaweed.

Terns tend to have white bodies with grey backs and wings, very often a black cap and sometimes a jaunty crest. Their bills and feet range in colour from black to blood-red or yellow. Exceptionally aerial, they roost at night but are in the air for most of the day, outside the breeding season. They can live for long periods on the wing. They fly with steady purposeful wingbeats, never soaring, tending to look down, their beaks pointing to the water. In searching for fish they may hover, then plunge head first for small fish at the surface – splash, snatch and up again.

Terns will normally have paired before they reach the nesting quarters but courting continues with highly ritualised displays which include ceremonial feeding.

Typically, terns nest in close-packed colonies, some very populous indeed. The stimulus and noise of company leads them to synchronise their egg-laying, with resulting advantages in terms of safety – the safety of numbers which confuses predators like rats, skuas and gulls. Even so, there is high mortality, which accounts for the average clutch of three or four eggs.

The nest is often little more than a shallow depression, a hollow on a sandy or shingle beach, usually on an island. The chicks are fed on whole small fish, such as sand-eels, which may be longer than the chick itself, so that while the head end is being digested the tail hangs out for all to see. Breeding success relies on the supply of suitable fish. The chicks are heavily dependent on their parents until long after they have fledged, but if they are lucky they may live to the ripe old age of 30.

ARCTIC TERN

Sterna paradisaea

In winter plumage

Length
33–38cm
(13–15in)

Wingspan
79–81cm
(31–32in)

Though they breed in the high Arctic summer, Arctic terns 'winter' in the austral summer, thus living a life of perpetual summer and almost endless daylight by travelling 20,000 miles a year: the only northern breeding species which migrates regularly to Antarctic waters. Seen around the pack-ice their crimson beaks have lost their colour – they are of course in winter plumage with white foreheads and lacking their long tail streamers. But beware of non-breeding Antarctic terns which also display white foreheads, though fortunately they also have a smoky-grey breastband to separate them from the northern visitors.

The Weddell Sea seems to be a staging area for feeding and moulting Arctic terns.

ANTARCTIC TERN

(Wreathed tern)
Sterna vittata

Length
41cm (16in)
Wingspan
79cm (31in)

The Antarctic tern closely resembles the Arctic tern, but the breeding adult – seen in the austral summer – is naturally in summer plumage, with a black cap and long tail streamers. Both have blood-red bills and red legs. Unlike the visiting Arctic terns, the Antarctic tern is resident and sedentary. Circumpolar and abundant in the peninsula, it is not a ship-follower.

The birds plunge-dive in typical tern fashion along the edge of the sea for small fish like the Antarctic herring and for crustaceans like krill.

From a few to a few dozen pairs, Antarctic terns nest colonially, not far from the sea. A mere scrape of natural saucer shape is decorated with a few desultory bits of vegetation or limpet shells. The birds are not faithful to their breeding grounds, which may change from season to season. Nesting takes place early, with eggs laid from mid-November. Clutch size is one or two; incubation is by both parents for 23 days, with the chicks hatching at two-day intervals from early December to late February. Both parents brood and feed. The chicks leave the nest to hide when they are three or four days old. They are fully fledged at 25 days, but remain cared for by the parents for some time.

Antarctic terns are much predated upon by skuas.

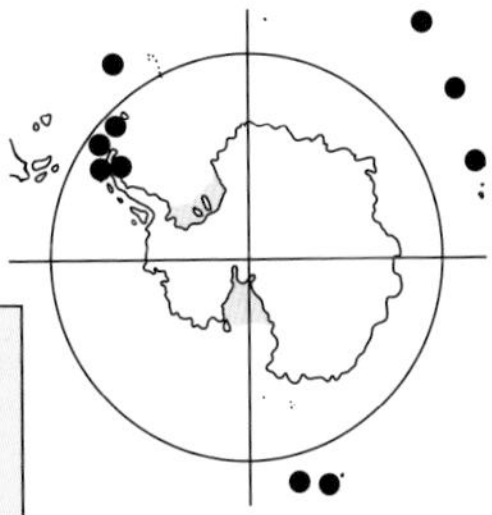

AURORA AUSTRALIS (SOUTHERN LIGHTS)

'Swaying auroral light ... fold on fold the arches and curtains of vibrating luminosity rise and spread across the sky, to slowly fade and yet again spring to glowing life.'

Robert Falcon Scott, *Journal*, June 1911

Ghostly flickerings and patterns of light, draperies of reds to violets and greens, subtly fill the winter sky, rising and falling in intensity. Best seen around the Ross Sea area and the coast of east Antarctica, and among the most beautiful of natural phenomena, the Aurora takes the form of arcs and beams of pulsating and flickering coloured lights quivering and shimmering and filling the upper sky, in the style of a fluorescent screen. The curtains and draperies of colour may be a mix of yellows, greens, violets and flaming reds, though green auroras are the most common. Even in high summer there is a fair chance of seeing the effect, though it will be confined to smoky blacks and greys sweeping across the sky.

(The ship *Aurora* was a 600-ton sealer from Dundee, under Captain John Davies. She served Douglas Mawson's expedition when he charted 2,000 miles of the Australian Antarctic in 1911–13.)

BIRDS OF SOUTH GEORGIA

Yellow-billed pintail
(South Georgia pintail,
South Georgian teal,
Brown or Chilean pintail)
Anas georgica

Speckled teal
Anas flavirostris

South Georgia pipit
Anthus antarcticus

South Georgia is home for prodigious numbers of birds (including all those recorded in this book except for the emperor and Adélie penguins). Thirty breeding and 27 non-breeding species have been recorded as occurring naturally; at least nine have been introduced. Most are seabirds, of course, but there are five established terrestrial and freshwater species.

The South Georgia pipit *Anthus antarcticus* is the only passerine bird in the Antarctic. On islands which are free from rats it is fairly common, living on insects and spiders in the summer, tideline debris items in the winter. Its song somewhat resembles that of the skylark.

There are two waterfowl. The yellow-billed pintail *Anas georgica* is a large, slender, mottled brown dabbling duck with striking yellow sides to the bill and a prominent pointed tail. (It replaces the northern pintail in South America, where it is widespread.) It feeds on algae in freshwater ponds in the summer and sheltered bays in the winter.

The speckled teal *Anas flavirostris* is a South American species which found its way to South Georgia in the 1960s, found only in the area of Cumberland Bay. It also has yellow sides to the bill, but is smaller and stockier than the pintail, with a dark head and short tail.

Although in geographical terms South Georgia is a sub-Antarctic island, its position south of the Convergence makes it biologically Antarctic.

INTRODUCED MAMMALS

The only mammals native to South Georgia are the seals and whales, but there have been the inevitable introductions. Both brown rats and house mice were brought to the island by sealers, probably arriving with the earliest explorers in the early 18th century. More deliberate and later introductions were cats and rabbits, but these have failed to establish wild populations because of the severe winter weather. Perhaps the most surprising encounter on present-day South Georgia is with the reindeer *Rangifer tarandus*, which was first imported in November 1911 by the Norwegian whaling companies to provide both sport and fresh meat. The original three stags and seven hinds, plus later imports, produced descendants which have flourished and expanded their range. The numbers are effectively controlled by the availability of tussock, which is rich in carbohydrates. There are now some 2,000 individuals in the island's two separate populations. Recently calves have been taken from Husvik and introduced to East Falkland.

SEALS

Fur seal skeleton

True seal skeleton

There are two main divisions – Superfamilies – in the Pinnipeds. First the Otariidae which includes fur seals, sea lions and walruses. In the Antarctic, the only representative of these 'eared' seals is the fur seal *Arctocephalus gazella*. They have pointed snouts, a very thick underfur and hind flippers which can be turned forwards and used to great effect in almost galloping over land.

The other major grouping is of the Phocidae, the 'true' seals which have no protruding external ear, cannot run or raise themselves on fore flippers, cannot swivel their hind flippers and must clumsily haul or hump themselves on land in caterpillar fashion.

Seals are well adapted to aquatic life in polar regions, cushioned and insulated from the cold air as effectively as from cold water with either a thick coat of blubber or a dense pelage.

They have torpedo-shaped bodies superbly designed for fast underwater travel. Their nostrils may be closed and sealed by muscular contraction as they enter the water. They exhale before diving to reduce the amount of air in their lungs and derive the necessary oxygen from their well-supplied blood systems. Their heart-rate slows, their metabolism is reduced. On surfacing it is several minutes before their heart-beat returns to its surface rate.

Seals must come ashore to breed, but some species are as comfortably able to pup on the fast-ice as on the sub-Antarctic or continental beaches.

Males and pregnant females gather annually at the breeding place, where copulation takes place soon after the pups are born. Implantation is delayed for three months so that, although the gestation period is nine months, the annual cycle is maintained.

Killer whales are among their natural enemies, but the exploitation for skins and blubber which followed the discovery of the abundance of Antarctic seal stocks in the 18th century brought populations to near extinction within 150 years. In response to protection, stocks are currently recovering spectacularly.

The four truly Antarctic species are the leopard, the crabeater, the Weddell and the Ross seal. The Antarctic fur seal and the southern elephant seal, or sea elephant, the largest of all the seals, are abundant elsewhere in the sub-Antarctic islands and southern South America, but are at the southern end of their range in the Antarctic Peninsula.

Sea bear (the common fur-seal of commerce). Engraving from Jardine's 'The Naturalist's Library', 1839

SEAL TERMINOLOGY
A non-breeding gathering of seals is known as a *herd*, breeding seals form a *rookery*. Bull seals maintain cow seals in a *harem*. The newborn is a *pup*, groups of pups form a *pod*. At four or five months old the pups become *yearlings*. Immature males are *bachelors*.

ANTARCTIC FUR SEAL

(Southern fur seal, Kerguelen fur seal)
Arctocephalus gazella

Length
2m (6ft 6in)
Weight
males 90–115kg (200–250lb); females smaller

As fur seals go, the Antarctic is of medium size, the female being smaller than the male. Long guard hairs protect a dense and valuable underfur which traps a layer of air and provides thermal insulation. As a consequence, fur seals do not have such a well-developed thickness of blubber as the true seals.

They are greyish-brownish in colour, with a creamy throat and breast and a ginger belly. Mature males are a grizzled dark grey-brown above, paler below. The pup is born with a black coat. The not infrequent leucistic individuals are known as 'blondies'. The flippers are highly vascular, serving to radiate heat when the animals are active ashore, but conserving it when they are tucked into the body. Like all fur seals, their hind flippers can be deployed facing forwards or backwards, so that while they are able to propel themselves reasonably efficiently in the sea they are also able to walk and run on the land in a decidedly lively fashion. So be sure to give them a wide berth because they can charge across a beach faster than you can and they have an aggressive demeanour.

As moderately deep divers, working in the top 50m (165ft) of the sea, they take mainly krill but prey on fish, squid and, to a certain extent, penguins. Antarctic fur seals colonise isolated rocks and islets on oceanic islands south of the Convergence (a different species, *A. tropicalis*, occurs to the north).

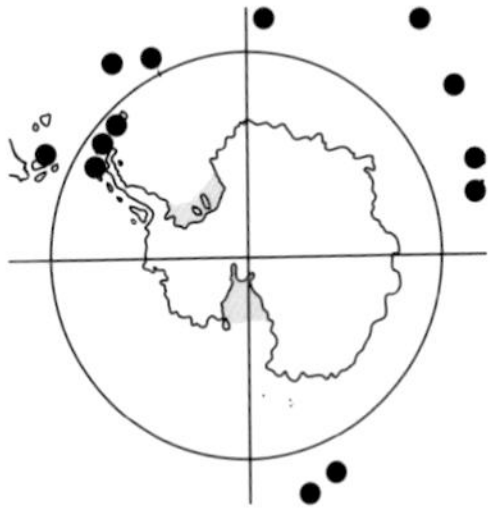

Adult males haul ashore and establish territories in late September, encouraging females to gather in a jealously guarded harem of up to half a dozen. The black furry pups are born from late November to mid-December. Eight days after their birth the bull mates with the female, the development of the embryo being delayed for three months before a gestation period of nine months, thus ensuring a 12-month cycle.

The generic name Arctocephalus is from the Greek, 'bear-headed'. Early mariners called them 'sea bears'.

During this period immature and non-breeding seals keep well out of harm's way at the edge of the breeding area or suffer in hard-fought encounters with the dominant bulls.

The pups, less than half a metre long and weighing only 5kg at birth, grow fast on a rich diet of creamy milk. Birth weight is doubled in about ten weeks. They are fed for up to 12 weeks before being abandoned to make their own way in the world.

From about February, the adults go into moult, completing their renewed pelage by the end of April in time for the austral winter.

Antarctic fur seals migrate northwards to warmer waters in the winter. After the horrific depredations of the early 19th century, when the species was brought almost to extinction, it is now increasing mightily under the protection of legislation. The main population, possibly four million, is on South Georgia but healthy numbers are also flourishing further south on the South Orkneys, South Sandwich and South Shetlands, as well as on Bouvet and Heard. Some may breed on Kerguelen, the island which gave one of their alternate names.

CRABEATER SEAL

(White seal)
Lobodon carcinopha

Length
2.6m (8ft 6in)
Weight
225kg (500lb); females slightly larger

The most abundant seal in the world, with a total population estimated at more than 15 million, the crabeater seal has a dog-like face and lightly spotted silvery tan pelage, dark brown above, blonde below. The flippers are dark. Numerous scars on the flanks and neck are presumably inflicted by leopard seals. The pelage fades to a creamy white in the summer, to be moulted in January to a darker coat, but older animals become progressively paler.

Crabeaters are slim and lithe, moving fast over the ice, able to sprint at speeds up to 25km/h (15mph), as fast as a fit young man.

Crabeater seals do not eat crabs! They eat krill and other crustaceans. No one seems able to give a credible reason for the English name. They catch krill by engulfing a shoal with open mouth, then forcing the water out between the sieve formed by their complicated – *pentacospid* – cheek teeth, retaining and swallowing the catch. They are said to consume 20–25 times their body weight of krill in a year, which might mean that the total population of crabeaters in the Antarctic takes 100 million tonnes of the standing stock of krill annually. In fact their numbers have increased healthily as a consequence of commercial whaling having reduced the stock of great whales in these waters.

Crabeaters are creatures exclusively of the pack-ice, well south of the Convergence, but only in areas where they have easy access to plenty of open water. They are especially abundant in the coastal waters of Graham Land and in the southern part of the Ross Sea. They tend to lie on the floes either alone or in small groups of three or four.

Their pups are born in spring, between the middle of September and the beginning of November, with a soft greyish-brown natal coat. They grow fast, nourished with a high-fat milk over a period of possibly five weeks, when they moult into a diving suit and go to sea. Adults moult in January into the darker pelage.

Crabeaters are gregarious, circumpolar and pelagic with the drifting pack-ice. They tend to stay close to the edge of the pack on its annual movements: north in the austral winter, south in the austral summer. Although they have been seen occasionally in New Zealand, Tasmania, southern Australia and South America (the most northerly occurrence was South Africa), they are basically creatures of the pack-ice.

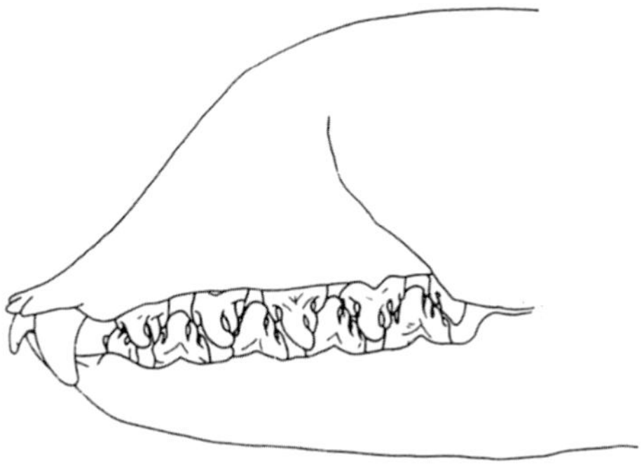

Cheek teeth of the crabeater seal. The lobes fit together to form a strainer to separate sea water from the krill that forms their food. (Leopard seals have a similar facility, but also larger canines for attacking crabeaters!)

WEDDELL SEAL

Leptonychotes weddellii

Length: male to 3m (9ft 9in); female 3.3m (10ft 10in)
Weight around 450kg (990lb)

One of the largest of all seals, with a smiling small face on a big body, the corners of the mouth turned upwards, the Weddell seal has deep brown eyes and short whiskers. It is blue-black and spotted silver-grey after a moult, fading to rust-brown. The most southerly mammal in the world, it lives almost exclusively in the fast-ice as deep as 78°S. It is often found on shore, unlike the crabeater.

Sedentary, placid and approachable on the ice, Weddell seals are accomplished divers. They are well adapted with a large oxygen store which allows them long submersions. In shallow dives their heart-rate slows to 50%, in deeper dives it reduces to 75%. Underwater their metabolism is depressed. The result is that, although most dives last about 15 minutes, they are capable of staying underwater for well over an hour. Dives to 300–400m (984–1,312ft), even 750m (2,460ft), are common, and this is the depth at which the giant Antarctic cod *Notothenia coriiceps (neglecta)* can be found. These benthic fish, which may be 1.5m (5ft) long and weigh 70kg (154lb), make up 58% of the seal's catch, crustaceans and squid making up the balance. With an underwater cruising speed of about 5 knots, the seals are able to swim over distances of several kilometres from the breathing-hole.

While they will utilise tidal cracks as breathing places, they are perfectly capable of enlarging an opening by sawing at the ice with their forward-pointing upper incisors and canines as they swing the head from side to side. This facility allows them to overwinter in the deep south. Their lives last only as long as their teeth; nevertheless they may live to 12 years, the oldest recorded individual being 22 years of age. (Other seals may reach 40.)

Weddell seals are highly vocal underwater, singing in a series of trills and chirps, probably in connection with establishing a breeding territory, for while females are granted free passage, males are not so welcome.

Pregnant cows begin to gather at the traditional pupping areas in August at the northern end of the range, at South Georgia and Signy Island, with the peak of births at the end of the month. In the deep south, where they breed in latitudes as low as 78°, pupping peaks in late October. Twins are rare. At birth the pups weigh 27kg (60lb) but they fatten fast on a diet of mother's milk which becomes 42% fat after the first few days. At two weeks old they lose their grey natal coat and moult over a month into a coat similar to that of the adult. Almost from birth they spend time in the water; by seven weeks of age they can dive to 92m (300ft), staying under for five minutes. Lactation lasts six or seven weeks, but the pup soon begins to take krill. During this period the cow starves, giving the pup constant protective attention.

The cows come on oestrus when the pupping season is over and the rookery breaks up. The bulls meanwhile have been jealously guarding their breeding territory and are readily available. Cows become sexually mature in their third year and may continue to pup for nine.

While the adolescent pups may gather together for some time after the breeding season, the adults tend to a more solitary life. They do not indulge in long-distance migrations.

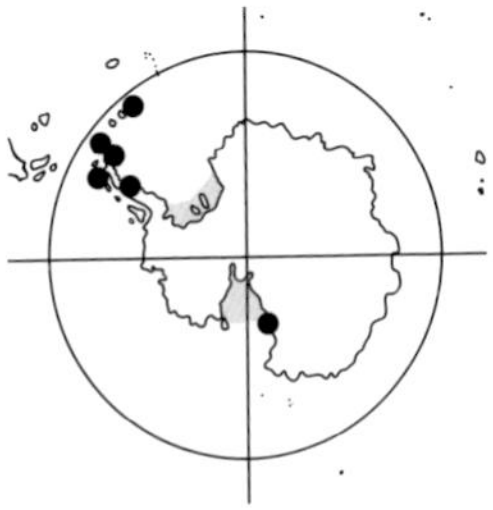

Weddell seals are the most southerly of all Antarctic seals. Apart from a small population in South Georgia they are associated with the ice. They are circumpolar and coastal, remaining on and under the fast-ice through the austral winter, patronizing tidal cracks or maintaining breathing holes in order to spend much time underwater. Movements are over relatively short distances and are presumably related to the availability of breathing holes.

LEOPARD SEAL

Hydrurga leptonyx

Average length: adult male 2.8m (11ft); adult female 2.9m (11ft 6in)
Average weight: adult male 325kg (715lb); adult female 370kg (810lb)

The spotted coat gives the leopard its name, but in looks its head is markedly snake-like, with a huge gape. Unlike the Weddell, its head seems too large for its sleek and slender body. The body is dark grey above and light grey below – the two shades clearly divided – with conspicuous 'leopard' spots on the throat, shoulders and sides.

The leopard seal is a solitary animal, but not particularly uncommon, especially near penguin colonies, though it ranges widely over the fringes of the pack and fast-ice.

Leopard seals are built for speed. They attend traditional landing and launching places by penguin colonies, then chase and catch penguins in the water, bringing them to the surface and shaking them so severely that they are turned inside out – and more conveniently eaten. But penguins are a small proportion of their diet. They are opportunist and catholic feeders, taking a wide variety of prey; probably a third of their catch is of fish and krill. They also take other seals, particularly the young crabeaters, leaving the ones which escape with scars corresponding to the spacing between their massive canine teeth. In the case of krill, they engulf a quantity, complete with seawater, then expel the water using their teeth as filters, before swallowing the catch in the style of crabeaters. Although they have a reputation for violence and aggressiveness, there seems little evidence that leopard seals will attack people, though there has been one horrendous accident. They have been known to puncture inflatable boats. They will certainly come to take a thoughtful look at anyone foolish enough to sit at the water's edge.

The pups are probably born between November and January and the lactation period is approximately two months: the pup suckles at an ice-floe haul-out.

Winter movements take them north to the sub-Antarctic islands (where many have bred) and as far as the coasts of South America, South Africa, southern Australia and New Zealand.

Killer whales are probably their only natural enemies; leopard seals have never been the subject of exploitation by man.

SOUTHERN ELEPHANT SEAL

(Sea elephant, sea wolf, proboscis seal)
Mirounga leonina

Length: males to 4.5m (14ft 6in); females to 2.8m (11ft)
Weight: males around 4,000kg (4 tonnes); females around 900kg (almost a tonne)

The southern elephant seal is the largest seal in the world today. Reversing the norm though, the bull is substantially larger than the cow. The name comes partly from the elephantine size but also from the extraordinary trunk-like proboscis of the bull, which is inflatable, and attains its full splendour when the animal is in its eighth year.

The bulls are dark-grey, somewhat lighter in the underparts, but in time the pelage fades to greyish-brown. Bulls exhibit a great deal of scarring around the neck, where their skin is exceptionally thick. Cows are smaller, browner and darker, with a pale effect around the neck resulting from many love-bites. Elephant seal hair is stiff and rough.

Their food consists mainly of squid plus 25% fish, caught in deep diving. Dives last in excess of 30 minutes and have been recorded to 1,000m (3,300ft). Cheek teeth are reduced to widely-spaced pegs, an adaptation associated with a squid diet. At sea, they gorge themselves and fatten so that their blubber reserves sustain them during the long breeding and moulting period ashore, during which they fast.

Pregnant cows come ashore on traditional beaches in September/October, hauling out a few days before the pup is born, in mid-October. The bulls are already on the beaches, establishing dominance amongst themselves and guarding a harem of somewhere between 28 and 53 cows. In establishing their territory they produce a bubbling roar of impressive loudness, aided by the resonating chamber of the proboscis. If there are too many cows for the 'beachmaster' to handle, then he will co-opt an assistant. But in response to continual challenges, ownership of a harem may well change hands. Most of the rumbustious behaviour is over by early December and the beaches become relatively quiet.

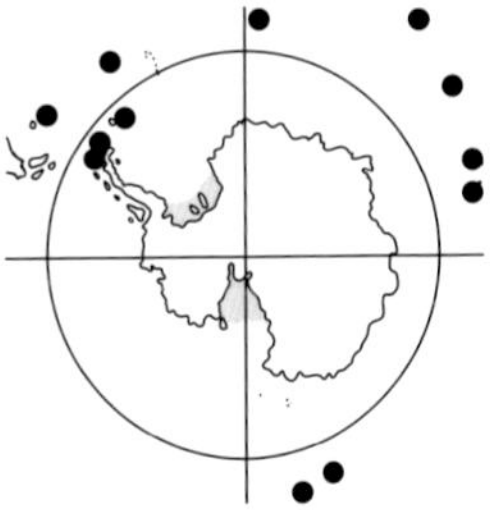

During the four weeks of lactation, pups gain 9kg (20lb) a day while the cow may lose as much as 135kg (300lb) in the process, starving all the time.

The cows are ready to mate again before the pup is fully weaned – and the beachmaster is on hand to perform. A cow may produce as many as seven pups in an average lifespan of 12 years. After serving the cows, the bulls return to the sea to feed. On weaning, the pups are abandoned, fast for a month and then find their way to the water to learn to swim and catch fish without help from the parents.

After a period of post-breeding feeding at sea, the adults return to the shore in late summer to gather at muddy and stinking wallows for the 40 days of moult. This is a time when their gregarious nature shows, for they lie closely side by side in close companionship – behaviour known as *thigmotaxis*. Bulls may live to an age of 20 years.

Elephant seals breed on sub-Antarctic islands, where they lie about on beaches and amongst the tussock. At the southern end of their range they must perforce endure a certain amount of snow and ice. On dispersal they go to sea, and travel widely.

Blubber
Elephant seal blubber may be over 15cm (6in) in thickness – oil-filled cells held in place by fibrous and elastic connecting tissue. It was this mass of blubber which brought the sealers to the Southern Ocean to kill the seals in such devastating numbers. By the late 18th century more than 100 vessels were engaged in securing seal oil in the Southern Ocean.

ROSS SEAL

Ommatophoca rossii

Length: average male 2m (6ft 6in); female 2.15m (7ft)

Weight: average male 175kg (380lb); female 190kg (410lb)

A graceful and slender seal with large head and thick neck, the Ross seal lives only in the dense pack. Until recently it was seen only rarely, but the arrival of powerful ice-breakers has opened up the heavy and consolidated pack and many more sightings are being recorded.

Dark above, it is sharply divided to silvery-grey below, with much streaking around the head, throat and sides. The eyes are the largest of any seal, in a wide head with short snout. Disturbed, it raises its head and leans back in an open-jawed posture, unlike any other seal. It has small conical teeth for grabbing squid. The presumption is that large squid are a major component of its diet, plus a smaller proportion of fish and krill.

The Ross seal is a solitary animal, living in one of the remotest of all habitats, and much of its life is only dimly understood. It is a very vocal seal, singing trills and arpeggios which carry over a great distance, so that its loneliness may be more apparent than real.

Ross seals are circumpolar within the interior region of dense pack-ice. Their pups are born in November.

The Ross seal was the last discovered and is the least known of all pinnipeds. Captain James Clark Ross found them at 68°S 176°E and collected two specimens during the British Antarctic Expedition of 1839–43 with HMS *Erebus* and HMS *Terror*.

WHALES

Whales, dolphins and porpoises are members of the order Cetacea. They are totally adapted to a life at sea but, as mammals, they must surface to breathe. Modifications to the standard mammal design involve a hairless fish-shape encased in a thick layer of insulating blubber, the nose on top of the head, forefeet becoming paddles, effective loss of hind feet and the tail becoming a horizontal fluke. Supported by water, they are free to grow to a great size and weight. They are divided into two broad sub-orders, the Odontoceti (toothed whales) and the Mysticeti (whalebone or baleen whales). Sperm and killer whales (which are large dolphins) and the other dolphins belong to the toothed division, and are beasts of prey, whereas the whalebone whales feed by filtering plankton through a series of baleen plates which hang from the position normally occupied by the upper teeth.

Working in murky water at great depths, toothed whales find their prey by echo-location, using ultrasonic pulses which are inaudible to human ears. They communicate within their group with trills, whistles, grunts and groans which are perfectly audible above water.

Baleen whales have a profoundly different method of feeding. In relatively shallow water, they plough through the concentrations of plankton (possibly finding them by taste), gulping great quantities of water, expelling it through filter-plates of whalebone by contracting the ventral grooves of the throat and pressing the large tongue against the roof of the mouth, then swallowing the catch of uncountable numbers of small shrimps and larval fish. Not needing the agility and manoeuvrability of the hunting whales, they enjoy the advantages of greater size: the blue whale is the largest animal ever to live on earth.

Hold your breath!

In diving, the blow-holes are firmly closed, and the heart-rate is slowed down. Whales are tolerant of a high concentration of carbon dioxide in the blood, which is plentifully supplied with myoglobin. The result is that they are able to hold their breath for periods which would drown land animals. The breathing passages are separated from the gullet so that they are able to feed underwater without choking.

SOUTHERN RIGHT WHALE

Eubalaena australis

Length
to 17m (58ft)
Weight
to 100 tonnes

Known as the right whale because it was the 'right' one to hunt, it is slow moving, therefore easy to harpoon, and is richly provided with oil so that it floats when dead, highly convenient in both respects for whalers. By the end of the 19th century the northern stocks were nearly exhausted, but under protection they are making a slow recovery.

The southern right whale is a robust black-brown whale, with a huge head. The lower lips reach up and fold over an arched rostrum. The two blow-holes are set apart and in front of them is a 'bonnet' of callosities. Others are arranged around the head in a way which is said to identify individual animals. The callosities are inhabited by whale lice (crustaceans) which give a white to pink to yellow-orange effect. The blow is high, busy and V-shaped. The flippers are large and broad, and there is no dorsal fin.

Southern right whales feed on krill in surface waters, shallow-diving for about 20 minutes, then cruising on the surface for 5–10 minutes, blowing about every minute. The population of these whales is much reduced as a result of excessive exploitation, but they are occasionally seen around the South Shetlands and in the fjords of South Georgia. They are also associated with other sub-Antarctic islands such as Kerguelen and Crozet. They move north in the austral winter, many summering off the Valdez Peninsula in Patagonia. The total population may be in the order of several thousand.

Dive sequence for right whale. Note the V-shaped spout from the two blow-holes and especially the absence of a dorsal fin.

BLUE WHALE

Balaenoptera musculus

Length
to 30m (98ft)
Weight
to 150 tonnes

Called the blue whale because of the bluish-grey skin, *musculus* is variously taken to mean 'muscular', which makes sense, or as a diminutive of the Latin '*mus*' for mouse, which may just be an 18th-century Linnaean joke. It is the largest animal which has ever lived on earth.

The blue whale has a huge mottled metallic-blue-grey body, flat head, and small hook-shaped dorsal fin placed well back towards the slender and graceful fluke. Slow moving, with a straight and powerful vertical blow – not bushy – which may reach nearly 10m (33ft), especially in cold air. It generally breathes in shallow dives at 20-second intervals before diving for half an hour. After the spout, the long expanse of back rolls over, the small fin emerging just before the tail fin makes a brief appearance. Their surface cruising speed is about 3 or 4km/h (up to 2.5mph). They are easily spooked.

Blue whales travel solo or in groups of up to three or four but they may congregate at particularly rich feeding waters. In the Antarctic summer blue whales feed on krill, taking some 8,000kg (over 8 tonnes) in a day, which may amount to 8 million shrimps.

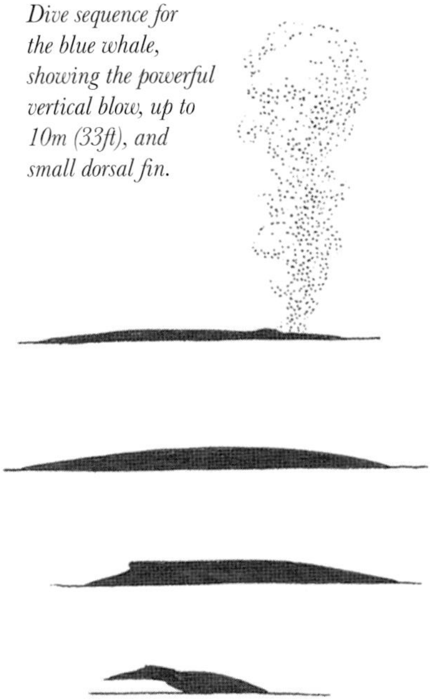

Dive sequence for the blue whale, showing the powerful vertical blow, up to 10m (33ft), and small dorsal fin.

When the pack-ice extends north at the onset of the Antarctic winter, blue whales in turn move north towards the warm tropical waters where they live off their blubber reserves and gather in discrete groups for courtship and mating at about ten years of age. (The male's penis is over 3m (10ft) long.)

The gestation period is nearly 12 months, thus the single calves are born in the warm waters in which they were conceived. They are nursed for more than six months, by which time they are over 15m (50ft) in length and they begin to take their share of the krill. They will be sexually mature when they reach 23m (75ft). Females probably breed every three years.

Gangs of killer whales have been seen to attack blue whales, biting at their flukes and mouth parts.

Blue whales are widely distributed throughout the seven seas, along shelf waters and the pack edge, but also in open waters. There are several discrete stocks, based on the North Pacific, North Atlantic and the southern hemisphere. Their numbers were devastated by ill-regulated whaling and progressively effective protection has so far failed to promote a real recovery. Their total world population may be in the region of 10,000.

FIN WHALE

(Finback, razorback)
Balaenoptera physalus

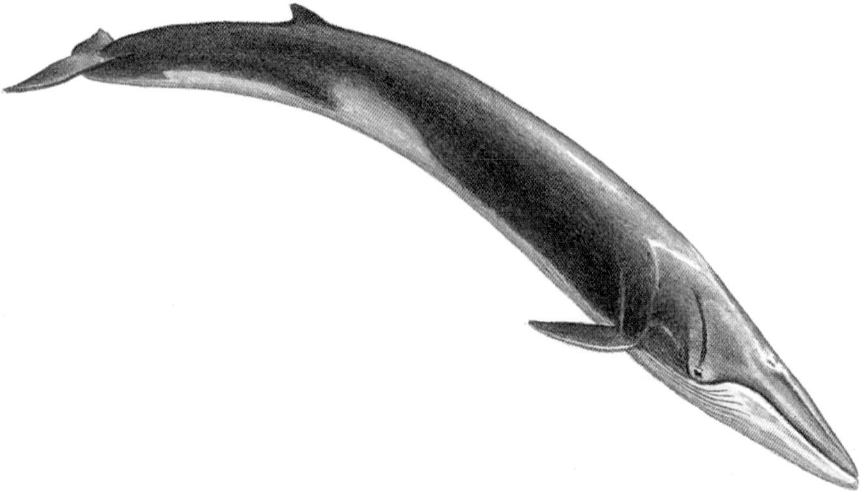

Length
to 27m (88ft)
Weight
to 90 tonnes

A regular summer visitor to the Antarctic, the fin whale is similar in shape to the blue – also a rorqual – but is smaller and with a larger dorsal fin (it is the prominent dorsal which gives it its common name). The rostrum is also narrower and more V-shaped than that of the blue. It is dark grey to brownish-black on back and sides, the back being ridged from the dorsal fin to the flukes (the 'razorback'). The underparts are white. Curiously, the head is dark on the port side and much paler on the starboard. Also on the starboard side the lower lip and baleen plates are yellowish-white while those on the port side are more blue-grey.

These irregularities are presumably connected with the way in which the animal scoops its plankton catch, when it rolls over on its side so that the starboard side becomes the undersurface and its mouth engulfs krill in a sideways fashion. It also deep-dives for fish and squid, reaching depths over 230m (750ft).

In leisurely surfacing, the blow comes first – a tall spout spraying to 6m (20ft) and blossoming at its full height – followed by a slow roll and the appearance of the fin, but not the tail. Four or five blows occur at intervals of 10–20 seconds, the final roll before the dive revealing more of the back and possibly the tail. In a deep dive the animal may be down for nearly half an hour.

They occasionally leap clear of the water in a breach. Often solitary, they may also travel in pairs or in small social groups. Fin whales are fast movers, able to cruise all day at a comfortable 7 knots but to sprint at 18 knots, a speed which saved them from the attention of the whalers until the arrival of fast catcher boats. When met in the open sea, they may choose to swim in company with a ship for a while, keeping station on the beam until they fall back.

Distribution of fin whales is worldwide. From the Antarctic they move north to the southwest Pacific as high as Peru and in the Atlantic to Brazil, to the west coast of South Africa and into the southern Indian Ocean.

With the advent of fast catchers, fin whales became a practical prey and the Antarctic populations were much reduced. Protected now, at least on paper, their population is conjectural.

Fin whale dive sequence showing the vertical blow, up to 6m (20ft). Tail flukes may not appear.

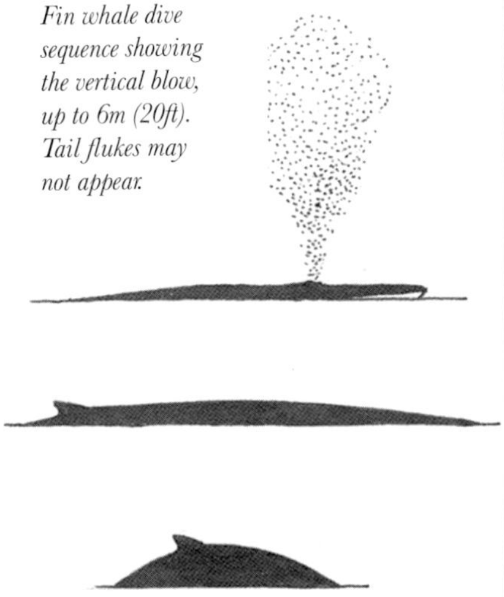

ANTARCTIC MINKE WHALE

(Piked whale, lesser rorqual)
Balaenoptera bonaerensis

Average length: males 8m (26ft); females 8.2m (27ft)
Maximum length 10.7m (35ft)
Average weight 5,800–7250kg (6–8 tonnes)
Maximum weight 10 tonnes

Smallest and most abundant of the rorquals, with a streamlined but perhaps less slender body than the larger relatives, the Minke whale has a narrow, pointed and triangular rostrum, with a ridge on top of a flat head. The upperparts are black, the underparts white from the chin back. There is pale grey blazing on the flanks, one above and behind the flippers and one in front of the fin. The tall, pointed dorsal fin is set well back on the body. The pectoral fin is light grey, sometimes with a distinct pale band – unlike the dark grey slashed with a white band of the more northern common Minke. They are found close inshore within the pack-ice, often many miles from open water.

Captain Minke was a Norwegian whaler who boasted of huge whales but actually captured small ones…

Minkes are fast, dolphin-like swimmers, travelling on the surface at speeds up to 16 knots. They are commonly attracted to vessels, keeping station or even diving from side to side. Since the early 1990s Minkes have steadily altered their behaviour. Whereas in those years they were regarded as somewhat diffident creatures which tended to ignore ships, these days they seem positively to welcome the chance to approach closely, to swim with ships and to show great interest in Zodiacs, chasing them, diving under them, spyhopping and even breaching alongside.

The blow is low and insubstantial, sometimes almost invisible; the animal often begins its blow before it has surfaced. Normally the breathing sequence involves five to eight blows at intervals of less than a minute, followed by a dive lasting perhaps 20 minutes. The fin surfaces with the blow. On diving, the tail stock is arched high, but the fluke does not appear. Sometimes they will breach clear of the water.

Minke whales are seen as anything from single animals to several, but in areas of plankton abundance there may be a feeding assembly of a thousand. They take plankton and also squid. In turn they may be attacked by killer whales.

Minke males are sexually mature when they reach a length of about 7.2–7.7m (24–25ft), and females 7.9–8.1m (26ft), and are seven or eight years old. Gestation is 10–11 months; the calves are weaned in six months. Circumpolar migratory movements are little known, but they travel north to equatorial waters to avoid the austral winter. Larger animals penetrate further south in the austral summer while non-breeders, calves and immatures remain north of 50°S.

The total world population may be in the order of half a million, of which perhaps 200,000 are in the Antarctic, where they are flourishing. As a consequence, they are taken by pelagic factory-whalers, mainly as meat for the Japanese market.

Dwarf Minke whale, Balaenoptera acutorostrata subspecies. This small version of the Antarctic Minke, as yet unrecognised taxonomically, has a striking white pectoral patch which extends to a shoulder patch above the flipper. It may reach a maximum 8.1m (26ft) in length.

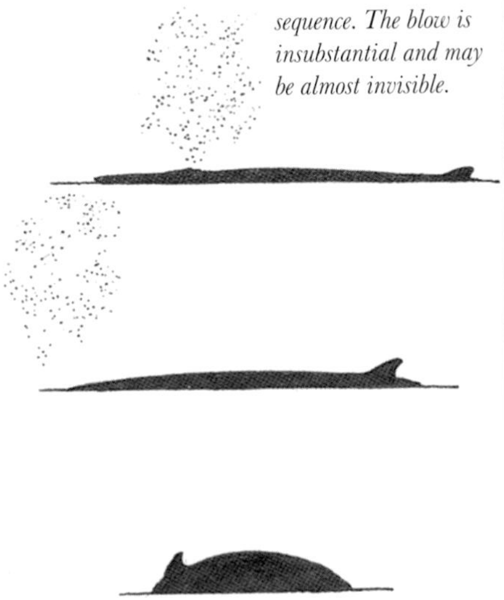

Minke whale dive sequence. The blow is insubstantial and may be almost invisible.

HUMPBACK WHALE

Megaptera novaeangliae

Length: male 15m (49ft); female 16m (52ft)
Weight to 48 tonnes

Send fluke pictures to Antarctic Humpback Whale Catalogue, Allied Whale, College of the Atlantic, Bar Harbour, Maine 04609, USA.

Underside of humpback tail fluke

A stoutly robust whale whose colour ranges from all-black or grey to black upperparts and white below. The head, lower jaws and chin are covered with fleshy knobs – tuberosities. The small dorsal fin sits on a raised hump (the humpback) with a series of smaller bumps leading to the tail. The most striking feature is the extraordinarily long pectoral flippers, nearly a third of the body length, some 5m (16ft) long. The flippers are white or nearly white; both they and the tail flukes are irregularly scalloped at the edges; the pigmentation pattern on the underside of the fluke is unique to the individual. This has made it possible for a catalogue of named individuals to be established (see address in margin).

They cruise slowly, at 4–6 knots, but are powerful enough to leap clear of the water frequently in spectacular breaching. The blow is bushy and reaches to 3m (10ft). They normally blow half a dozen times, and not more than ten, at 15–30-second intervals on surfacing in a feeding session. In diving, their flukes rise high above the surface. They may occasionally 'lobtail', bringing the tail down explosively on to the surface, presumably as some form of warning. They are highly vocal, whistling and rumbling in songs which are varied and intricate and are clearly designed for long-distance communication. As baleen whales, the Antarctic herds feed on crustaceans in the plankton. Their feeding technique is simply to engulf the krill swarms, either just under the surface or by lunging up to them from below. (It is in Alaskan waters that they have perfected the 'bubblefeeding' method, where they swim in an upward spiral, corralling and concentrating small fish inside a curtain of bubbles.) Often one of the long flippers rises above the surface in one of the surface lunges.

Humpback whales have a bushy blow, up to 3m (10ft), and raise their tail flukes well above the surface before diving.

Humpback whales normally breed every two years. After a 12-month gestation the single calf is born weighing a tonne and a half and over 4m (13ft) long. Humpbacks travel mostly in small groups, but may congregate in herds of a dozen or so. They are coastal animals, moving along predictable migration routes. Given that they are also slow moving, this made them easy prey in the old whaling days, with the result that their world stocks are now sadly depleted and slow in recovery.

In Antarctic waters there may be half a dozen discrete groups, summering on the krill-rich coastal waters, then moving north, each to its separate destination, to winter off the coasts of America, South Africa, western Australia and New Zealand.

Apart from man, their main enemy is the killer whale. They are usually infested with whale lice and host large numbers of tropical barnacles which duly perish in the cold water.

SPERM WHALE

(Cachalot)
Physeter macrocephalus

Average length: males 15m (50ft); females 11m (36ft)
Average weight: males 40 tonnes; females 22 tonnes

Once the main quarry of whalers (*vide Moby Dick*), the sperm whale is large and unmistakable, dark grey, sometimes blotched white, with a huge boxy head more than a third of its length, on top of a narrow underslung jaw which seems out of proportion – the classic 'great whale' of literature and illustration. (*White* sperm whales – as in *Moby Dick* – do occur, but are rare.) It has no dorsal fin, but two thirds of the way down the back there is a marked dorsal hump, followed by a series of knuckles reaching to the tail. Flippers are short. On surfacing, the massive head exposes the blow-hole, which is placed well on the port side, resulting in a biased blow which is characteristically well off centre and forward in direction. The offset blow is unique to sperm whales. The blow is explosive and can be heard at a great distance.

Most dives last about ten minutes followed by about ten blows at intervals of 10–15 seconds, but dives can extend to well over an hour. In sounding, they roll to reveal the hump and then lift the tail fluke high into the air in the manner of a humpback. They normally surface in the same place as they sound, the dive taking place vertically down and up.

The surface cruising speed is about 3 knots; on a dive it increases to 4 knots going down, then on the upward journey it reaches 5 knots. In search of giant squid, sperm whales dive regularly to 1,000m (3,281ft). They have been tracked by sonar to nearly 3,000m (9,843ft) – a bottom-dwelling shark was taken from a whale stomach where the depth was more than 3,200m (10,500ft). It is possible that the brilliantly white interior of the whale's mouth, in conjunction with the carmine tongue, acts as a lure, the whale simply opening its mouth and waiting for fish and squid to enter the trap. They eat up to a tonne each day. Around their heads they often have circular scars, sucker marks from the tentacles of the giant squid.

Sperm whales are widely distributed throughout the seven seas, always in deep water, but only the males penetrate into polar waters, in the summertime, when they may be found right up to the pack-ice but not inside it. They are often alone, sometimes in small groups.

Factory-ship whaling is now prohibited but sperm whales are still taken for shore stations from Iceland and to Japan. Their products of oil, spermaceti and meal go mainly to industry.

SPERMACETI

Spermaceti is a clear liquid wax which is found in the 'melon' – the massive forehead of the animal. It is contained in a 'case', and together they serve as a hydrostatic device which controls buoyancy. It is also speculated that the curious arrangements in the sperm whale's head associated with the spermaceti act as a kind of acoustic parabolic reflector, and that the undoubtedly violent noises this whale can produce may be used to stun their prey.

Taken from the whale and cooled, spermaceti sets as a white wax which accounts for the analogy with semen (spermaceti translates literally as 'whale semen').

AMBERGRIS

Ambergris is a pliable yellowy-brown wax-like substance which forms around squid beaks in the stomach of the sperm whale, rather in the manner of a hairball. Lighter than water, it melts at about 65°C and dissolves readily in absolute alcohol or vegetable oils. It has been used for centuries as a vehicle to retain and prolong the scent of perfume. Long prized as an aphrodisiac in the orient, its use in expensive perfumes (although synthetics are available) is logical enough.

ARNOUX'S BEAKED WHALE

Berardius arnuxii

Length to 9m (30ft)
Weight approximately 8 tonnes

The chances of seeing this whale are not great. Not many more than a couple of dozen have been closely examined, and these only as a result of strandings. They surface without fuss and the blow is discreet. The most noticeable feature is the bulb-shaped melon (forehead) and the long tube-like snout. The lower jaw is undershot and there are two pairs of teeth at its tip.

Upperparts are dark grey/brown/black, with pale patches and with white criss-cross scars inflicted in encounters with other members of the species. A small dorsal fin is situated two-thirds of the way between head and tail.

Little is known of the life of Arnoux's beaked whale at sea. It has been recorded in deep water around the peninsula and South Georgia, but most strandings have been in the New Zealand area.

SOUTHERN BOTTLENOSE WHALE

Hyperoodon planifrons

Like Arnoux's beaked whale, this species looks like a giant dolphin with an exaggeratedly large forehead. As in Arnoux's, the lower jaw is undershot, but not so markedly, and with only one pair of teeth.

The upperparts are grey/black and may be scored with tooth marks. Old males may have white heads. The hooked dorsal fin is set two-thirds of the distance between head and tail. The bushy forward blow reaches 2m (6ft).

Southern bottlenose whales occur in pods of a few animals or as lone individuals. They are deep divers, taking squid and pelagic fish. They are curious and may approach ships and lie alongside for a while.

Length approximately 9m (30ft)

Weight approximately 3 tonnes, up to 4.5 tonnes

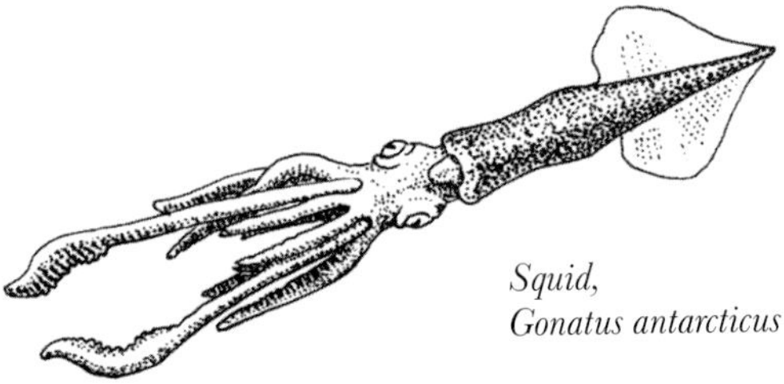

Squid, Gonatus antarcticus

SEI WHALE

(Sardine whale, coalfish whale)
Balaenoptera borealis

Length: males to 13–19m (43–62ft); females to 14–21m (46–69ft)

Weight: 15–30 tonnes

Pronounced 'say', from the Norwegian 'sejval', the name 'sei' is said to derive from the whale's appearance on the northern fishing grounds at the same time as the 'sej'- coalfish and pollack (both fishes and whale are in pursuit of the same plankton animals). Halfway in size between the blue and the Minke, sei whales are a steely dark grey in colour, uniform either side of the head, which distinguishes them from the larger fin whale. Distribution is from tropical to sub-polar waters. They tend to be seen in deep water, sometimes in the northern part of the Drake Passage for instance, sometimes near the ice edge, but unpredictably, some years more than others.

A single ridge runs from the blowhole to the dorsal, which is relatively tall and strongly hooked. The back is likely to be scarred with oval marks caused by cookie-cutter shark bites. The blow and the dorsal appear together, the blow being tall and columnar much as in the case of the fin, but only to 3m (9ft), ie: less high and less dense.

Sei whales have a catholic diet, taking shrimps, copepods, amphipods, small fish and squid, ploughing steadily along the surface to engulf their prey, rather than lunging and gulping. As an adaptation to filtering copepods, they have finer hairs inside the baleen than other rorquals. In diving, they are straight-backed; the flukes are straight-edged with a conspicuous notch.

Much persecuted in the 1940s and 1960s, after the stocks of blue and fin whales were reduced, sei whales are now an endangered species.

HOURGLASS DOLPHIN

(Sea skunk)
Lagenorhynchus cruciger

Length
to 1.7m (5½ft)
Weight
to 100kg (220lb)

Strikingly marked in black and white, the hourglass dolphin has an all black body, except for the sides and belly which are white, squeezed black amidships to create an hourglass effect. Robustly built, with a short beak and a prominent dorsal fin, it is tall and sickle-shaped.

Hourglass dolphins regularly swim in groups of half a dozen to several dozen, often in company with larger whales. They are enthusiastic and acrobatic bow-riders and they are commonly seen south of the Antarctic Convergence, even to the edge of the pack in the Antarctic summer. They are the most southerly of all dolphins, circumpolar but markedly pelagic.

NB Peale's and Commerson's dolphins are the common species in Falkland waters, north of the Convergence.

KILLER WHALE

(Orca, demon dolphin, blackfish, fat chopper)
Orcinus orca

Orcinus – bringer of death
Orca – sea monster

Length: males to 9m (30ft); females to 8m (26ft)
Weight: males to 7 tonnes; females to 3½ tonnes

The largest dolphin, with a blunt head (lacking the rostrum, or beak, of many of the dolphins), the classic killer whale is strikingly jet black above and brilliant white below, with a grey saddle behind the dorsal fin, a diagnostic white ellipse behind and above the eye and a white incursion from the belly into the flanks behind and below the saddle. The dorsal fin is highly distinctive: in the female it is often sickle-shaped and stands tall, but in the male it is triangular and reaches to almost 2m (over 6ft) and is unmistakable, even from a great distance.

Antarctic killer whales belong to one of three distinctive groupings. The first has the classic colouring, described above and found all around the world. The other two populations are similar but are grey instead of black. They differ in the size of their eye patches – one large and one small. Both have a characteristic 'dorsal cape' – a darker area over the back, extending from the eye patch to saddle patch.

In the Antarctic killers tend to travel in groups which are typically led by a dominant female, a matriarch. Adult males are usually closely related to the matriarch and do not breed within the group. Group size may range from a few to a couple of dozen or more.

They are curious and interested in ships, likely to change course and approach to cavort around and under a vessel which behaves with respect. They may also display interest by ‘spyhopping’ – rising vertically in the water as high as their paddle-shaped flippers in order to view the scene and search for likely prey. They may slap the water with their tails – ‘lobtailing’. Breaching’ clear of the water is behaviour common elsewhere but not yet recorded in the Antarctic. They can swim at great speed on the surface, though normally they cruise as a close-knit group, often in line abreast. They dive for several minutes, followed by a breathing sequence of 10–30 second shallow dives.

The name ‘killer’ landed them with an undeservedly vicious reputation in the past, though they are indeed predators on penguins, seals, fish and, on occasion, other whales. In the peninsula region they have taken minkes. There are no records of them taking scientists or even tourists, yet, though they are perfectly capable of tipping an ice floe over in order to topple an unwary crabeater seal into their jaws. They hunt co-operatively. Killer whales are a cosmopolitan and common species, found in coastal areas throughout the oceans. The Antarctic populations are commonly at home amongst the pack-ice, especially near the penguin rookeries which also attract seals.

Clear photos showing dorsal fins, saddle and/or eye patches will be much appreciated and acknowledged by the Antarctic Killer Whale Identification Catalogue. Sighting sheets from P O Box 1233, Whangarei, New Zealand. www.orcaresearch.org

Male killer whales leading a group

Dafila Scott

GLOSSARY OF SNOW AND ICE

Anchor ice Submerged ice which is attached to the bottom.

Bergy bit A piece of floating ice, generally showing less than 5m (16ft) above sea level but more than 1m (3ft), and normally about 10m (32ft) across.

Bight An extensive crescent-shaped indentation in the ice edge, formed either by wind or current.

Brash ice Accumulations of floating ice made up of fragments not more than 2m (6ft) across the wreckage of other forms of ice.

Calving The breaking away of a mass of ice from an ice wall, ice front, or iceberg.

Crevasse A fissure formed in a glacier; often hidden by snow bridges.

Fast-ice Sea-ice which forms and remains fast along the coast, where it is attached to the shore, to an ice wall, to an ice front, over shoals or between grounded icebergs. May extend a few metres or several hundred kilometres from the shore. May be more than one year old. When surface level is higher than 2m (6ft) above sea level it is called an ice shelf.

Firn Old snow which has recrystallised into a dense material.

Floe Floating ice other than fast-ice or glacier ice.

Frazil ice Fine spicules or plates of ice, suspended in water.

Frost smoke Fog-like clouds due to contact of cold air with relatively warm water, which can appear over openings in the ice or leeward of the ice edge, and which may persist while ice is forming.

Glacier A mass of snow and ice continuously moving to lower ground or, if afloat, continuously spreading.

Grease ice A later stage of freezing than frazil ice when the crystals have coagulated to form a soupy layer on the surface. Grease ice reflects little light, giving the sea a matt appearance.

Growler A piece of ice almost awash, smaller than a bergy bit.

Hummock A mound or hillock of broken floating ice forced upwards by pressure. May be fresh or weathered. The submerged volume of broken ice under the hummock, forced downward by pressure, is a bummock.

Iceberg A massive piece of ice of greatly varying shape, protruding more than 5m (16ft) above sea level. Icebergs may be described as tabular, dome-shaped, sloping, pinnacled, weathered or glacier bergs.

Ice blink A white glare on the underside of low clouds, indicating the presence of pack-ice or an ice sheet.

Icefoot A narrow fringe of ice attached to the coast, unmoved by tides and remaining after the fast-ice has broken free.

Lead A navigable passage through floating ice.

Moraine Ridges or deposits of rock debris transported by a glacier: lateral, along the sides; medial, down the centre; end, deposited at the foot.

Nilas A thin crust of floating ice, easily bending on waves and swell and rafting under pressure. It has a matt surface and is up to 10cm (4in) thick. Under 5cm (2in) it is dark, more than 5cm (2in), lighter.

Nip Ice is said to nip when it forcibly presses against a ship. A vessel so caught, though undamaged, is said to have been nipped.

Nunatak A rocky crag or small mountain projecting from and surrounded by a glacier or ice sheet.

Old ice Sea-ice more than two years old, up to 3m (10ft) or more thick.

Pack-ice, open Composed of floes seldom in contact and with many leads. Ice cover 4/10 to 6/10.

close Pack-ice in which the concentration is 7/10 to 8/10, composed of floes mostly in contact.

very close Pack-ice in which the floes are tightly packed but not frozen together, with little sea water visible. Ice cover practically 10/10.

consolidated Pack-ice in which the concentration is 10/10. The floes are frozen together and no water is visible.

Pancake ice Predominantly circular pieces of ice from 30cm (12in) to 3m (10ft) in diameter, and up to about 10cm (4in) in thickness, with raised rims due to the pieces striking against each other. Formed from the freezing together of grease ice, slush or shuga, or the breaking up of ice rind or nilas.

Polynya Any water area in pack or fast-ice other than a lead, not large enough to be called open water.

Rafting Pressure process by which one floe overrides another; most commonly found in new and young ice.

Rotten ice Sea-ice which has become honeycombed in the course of melting and which is in an advanced state of disintegration.

Sastrugi Sharp, irregular ridges formed on a snow surface by wind erosion and deposition. The ridges are parallel to the direction of the prevailing wind.

Sea-ice Any form of ice found at sea which results from freezing sea water.

Shuga An accumulation of spongy white ice lumps, a few centimetres across, formed from grease ice or slush and sometimes from anchor ice rising to the surface.

Snow bridge An arch formed by snow which has drifted across a crevasse, forming first a corniche, and ultimately a covering which may completely obscure the opening.

Stranded ice Ice which has been floating and has been deposited on the shore by retreating high water.

Tabular berg A flat-topped iceberg. Most tabular bergs form by calving from an ice shelf and show horizontal banding.

Tongue A projection of the ice edge up to several kilometres in length, caused by wind or current.

CODE OF CONDUCT FOR VISITORS TO THE ANTARCTIC

Activities in the Antarctic are governed by the Antarctic Treaty of 1959 and associated agreements, referred to collectively as the Antarctic Treaty System. The treaty establishes Antarctica as a zone of peace and science. As the world's last great wilderness, it is particularly vulnerable to human presence. Life in Antarctica must contend with one of the harshest environments on earth, and we must take care that our presence does not add more stress to this fragile and unique ecosystem. These guidelines were prepared by IAATO – the International Association of Antarctic Tour Operators – in the interests of conservation. See also www.iaato.org.

1 Protect Antarctic Wildlife

Taking or harmful interference with Antarctic wildlife is prohibited except in accordance with a permit issued by a national authority.

- Do not use aircraft, vessels, small boats, or other means of transport in ways that disturb wildlife, either at sea or on land.
- Do not feed, touch, or handle birds or seals, or approach or photograph them in ways that cause them to alter their behaviour. Special care is needed when animals are breeding or moulting.
- Do not damage plants, for example by walking, driving, or landing on extensive moss beds or lichen-covered scree slopes.
- Do not use guns or explosives. Keep noise to the minimum to avoid frightening wildlife.
- Do not bring non-native plants or animals into the Antarctic such as live poultry, pet dogs and cats or house plants.

2 Respect Protected Areas

A variety of areas in the Antarctic have been afforded special protection because of their particular ecological, scientific, historic or other values. Entry into certain areas may be prohibited except in accordance with a permit issued by an appropriate national authority. Activities in and near designated Historic Sites and Monuments and certain other areas may be subject to special restrictions.

- Know the locations of areas that have been afforded special protection and any restrictions regarding entry and activities that can be carried out in and near them.
- Observe applicable restrictions.
- Do not damage, remove, or destroy Historic Sites or Monuments or any artifacts associated with them.

3 Respect Scientific Research

Do not interfere with scientific research, facilities or equipment.

- Obtain permission before visiting Antarctic science and support facilities; reconfirm arrangements 24–72 hours before arrival; and comply with the rules regarding such visits.
- Do not interfere with, or remove, scientific equipment or marker posts, and do not disturb experimental study sites, field camps or supplies.

4 Be Safe

Be prepared for severe and changeable weather and ensure that your equipment and clothing meet Antarctic standards. Remember that the Antarctic environment is inhospitable, unpredictable, and potentially dangerous.

- Know your capabilities, the dangers posed by the Antarctic environment, and act accordingly. Plan activities with safety in mind at all times.
- Keep a safe distance from all wildlife, both on land and at sea.
- Take note of, and act on, the advice and instructions from your leaders; do not stray from your group.
- Do not walk on to glaciers or large snow fields without the proper equipment and experience; there is a real danger of falling into hidden crevasses.
- Do not expect a rescue service. Self-sufficiency is increased and risks reduced by sound planning, quality equipment, and trained personnel.
- Do not enter emergency refuges (except in emergencies). If you use equipment or food from a refuge, inform the nearest research station or national authority once the emergency is over.
- Respect any smoking restrictions, particularly around buildings, and take great care to safeguard against the danger of fire. This is a real hazard in the dry environment of Antarctica.

5 Keep Antarctica Pristine

Antarctica remains relatively pristine, the largest wilderness area on Earth. It has not yet been subjected to large-scale human perturbations. Please keep it that way.

- Do not dispose of litter or garbage on land. Open burning is prohibited.
- Do not disturb or pollute lakes or streams. Any materials discarded at sea must be disposed of properly.
- Do not paint or engrave names or graffiti on rocks or buildings.
- Do not collect or take away biological or geological specimens or man-made artifacts as a souvenir, including rocks, bones, eggs, fossils, and parts or contents of buildings.
- Do not deface or vandalise buildings, whether occupied, abandoned, or unoccupied, or emergency refuges.

USEFUL WEBSITES AND ADDRESSES

American Polar Society apolars@presys.com

ANARE Club (Australian National Research Expeditions) www.anareclub.org.au

Antarctic digital database www.nerc-bas.ac.uk/public/magic/add_home.html

Antarctic geographic names www.pnra.it/scar_gaze

Antarctic Heritage Trust www.heritage-antarctica.org

Antarctic Killer Whale Identification Catalogue www.orcaresearch.com

Antarctica New Zealand www.antarcticanz.govt.nz

Australian Antarctic Division www.antdiv.gov.au

Birdlife International www.birdlife.org

British Antarctic Survey www.antarctica.ac.uk

Icecharts www.natice.noaa.gov/home.htm

International Association of Antarctic Tour Operators www.iaato.org

James Caird Society Dulwich College, London SE21 7LD (for fans of Shackleton)

List of Protected Areas www.nerc-bas.ac.uk/public/magic/protected-area

Montreal Antarctic Society mtl.ant.soc@simpatico.ca

New Zealand Antarctic Society marga@chch.planet.org.nz

Philately www.south-pole.com

Save the Albatross www.savethealbatross.org

Satellite pictures www.polar.org/sat_image

Scientific Committee on Antarctic Research www.scar.org

Scott Polar Research Institute www.spri.cam.ac.uk

South Georgia www.sgisland.org

US Antarctic Resource Center www.usarc.usgs.gov

US National Science Foundation www.nsf.gov/home/polar/start.htm

'An Antarctic expedition is the worst way
to have the best time of your life.'

The worst journey in the world,
Apsley Cherry-Garrard

FURTHER READING

Alexander, Caroline 1998 *The Endurance* Bloomsbury

Anon 1988 *Antarctica* Reader's Digest

Armstrong, T, *et al* 1973 *Illustrated Glossary of Snow and Ice* Cambridge

Bonner, W N and Walton, D W H (eds) 1985 *Antarctica* Pergamon Press

Carwardine, Mark 1995 *Whales and Dolphins – Eyewitness Guide* Dorling Kindersley

Croxall, J P *et al* 1987 *Seabirds: Feeding Ecology* Cambridge University Press

Fothergill, A 1993 *Life in the Freezer: A Natural History of the Antarctic* BBC Books

Gurney, Alan 1997 *Below the Convergence* Pimlico

Harrison, P 1983 (rev edn) *Seabirds, An Identification Guide* Croom Helm

Hart, Ian 2001 *Pesca, a history of modern whaling in the Antarctic* Aidan Ellis

Headland, R 1992 *The Island of South Georgia* Cambridge University Press

Headland, R 1993 *Chronological List of Antarctic Expeditions* Cambridge University Press

King, H G R *et al* 1994 *The Antarctic* World Bibliographical Series Vol 171 Clio Press, Oxford

Lewis Smith, R I 1984 Terrestrial plant biology of the sub-Antarctic and Antarctic. In *Antarctic Ecology*, 1, 61-162 Academic Press, London

Lockley, R M 1974 *Ocean Wanderers* David & Charles

Matthews, L H 1971 *The Life of Mammals* Weidenfeld and Nicolson

Murphy, R C 1936 *Oceanic Birds of South America* Macmillan

Parmelee, D F 1992 *Antarctic Birds* University of Minnesota Press

Ray, G C 1981 *Wildlife of the Polar Regions* Chanticleer Press

Reeves, R R *et al* 2002 *Sea mammals of the world* A&C Black

Ridgeway, S H and Harrison R J (eds) 1981 *Handbook of Marine Mammals* Academic Press, London

Shirihai, Hadoram 2002 *A complete guide to Antarctic wildlife* Alula Press

Rubin, Jeff 1996 *Antarctica* Lonely Planet

Soper, T 1989 *Oceans of Birds* David & Charles

Sparks, J and Soper, T 1987 *Penguins* David & Charles

Stonehouse, B 1990 *North Pole South Pole* Prion

Stonehouse, Bernard 2000 *The Last Continent* SCP Books

Tickell, W L N 2000 *Albatrosses* Yale University Press

Tickell, W L N 1994 *Atlas of Southern Hemisphere Albatrosses* University of Bristol

Williams, Tony D 1995 *Penguins* Oxford University Press

Woehler, E J (ed) 1993 *The Distribution & Abundance of Antarctic & Subantarctic Penguins* SCAR Cambridge

INDEX

AUTHOR

Tony Soper was co-founder of the BBC's famous Natural History Unit and became its first director-cameraman, making wildlife films worldwide. Author of a dozen successful books, he now leads expeditions to remote islands in search of seabirds, seals and great whales. He has crossed the Southern Ocean to the Antarctic peninsula and the continental coast well over a hundred times.

ILLUSTRATOR

Dafila Scott is an artist and zoologist, best known for her studies of birds and coral fish. She is a member of the Society of Wildlife Artists and has travelled extensively from the tropics to the Antarctic. Dafila is the daughter of the late ornithologist and painter Sir Peter Scott, and grand-daughter of Captain Robert Falcon Scott – 'Scott of the Antarctic'.

ACKNOWLEDGEMENTS

Books like this are only possible with a great deal of help! We particularly thank the following for their generosity: Rex Banks, Librarian of the Natural History Museum, London; Andrew Clarke, John Croxall, Chris Edwards, Ron Lewis Smith and Charles Swithinbank of the British Antarctic Survey; Norman Lasca of the University of Wisconsin; Kim Crosbie, Robert Headland, William Mills and Bernard Stonehouse of the Scott Polar Research Institute; Tony Martin of the Sea Mammal Research Unit; Michel Sallabery of the University of Santiago; Lance Tickell of the University of Bristol and Lars & Erica Wikander of Quark Expeditions.

We want to record our debt to other seagoing naturalists, many of whom have shared our polar excursions: Susan Adie, Sir David Attenborough, Mark Jones, Ronald Lockley, Mike Messick, Klemens Pütz, Tui de Roy, Darrel Schoeling, Sir Peter & Lady Scott, Keith Shackleton, Anna Sutcliffe, Frank Todd and Ingrid Visser. And like all seabird enthusiasts, we are greatly indebted to the pioneer works of Peter Harrison, whose *Seabirds: An Identification Guide* is the pelagic birders' bible.

None of our voyages would have been successful without the wholehearted co-operation and enthusiasm of those polar seamen who braved the roaring forties, the furious fifties and the screaming sixties to sail with the whales and the petrels and penetrate to the remotest Antarctic islands and the continent, landing us on the fast-ice and penguin-rich beaches. We think particularly of Captains Gennady Josephov of *Professor Molchanov*, Sergei Nesterov of *Professor Multanovskiy*, Filip Kolesnikov of *Professor Khromov*, Karl-Ulrich Lampe of *Endeavour*, Viktor Vasiliev of *Kapitan Khlebnikov*, Sergey Paschov of *Alla Tarasova* and Andrey Rudenko of *Lyubov Orlova*.

TS DS
April 2004